Klaus-Peter Fischer-Hellmann

Information Flow Based Security Control Beyond RBAC

How to enable fine-grained security
policy enforcement in business
processes beyond limitations
of role-based access control (RBAC)

Springer Vieweg

Dr. Klaus-Peter Fischer-Hellmann
Mühltal, Germany

ISBN 978-3-8348-2617-6   ISBN 978-3-8348-2618-3 (eBook)
DOI 10.1007/978-3-8348-2618-3

The Deutsche Nationalbibliothek lists this publication in the Deutsche Nationalbibliografie; detailed bibliographic data are available in the Internet at http://dnb.d-nb.de.

Library of Congress Control Number: 2012949281

Springer Vieweg

Printed on acid-free paper

Springer Vieweg is a brand of Springer DE. Springer DE is part of Springer Science+Business Media.
www.springer-vieweg.de

Foreword

The applicability of RBAC (role-based access control) for information flow control is limited. Business processes are used more and more for applications that imply control and information flows across inter-organisational and intra-organisational security domain boundaries. More fine-grained access control mechanisms than those offered by RBAC are necessary to enforce security policies of different domains involved without overly strict limitations. In this book, methods are introduced based on an analysis of security-relevant semantics of BPEL (Business Process Execution Language) that help to overcome the restrictions mentioned above. Semantic patterns implied by BPEL and Web services invoked are introduced in order to analyse and illustrate their relevance with respect to security policy-implied restrictions.

Procedures to apply the novel methods in practice are defined and a prototypical realisation of a tool for compliance assessment with security policies demonstrates the applicability of the approach.

Prof. Dr. Rainer Bischoff

June 2012

Preface

For a number of years now, Web Services Business Process Execution Language (WS-BPEL or BPEL for short) is broadly used for the definition of executable business processes. By exploiting the fact that BPEL is a platform-independent standard supported by several major vendors of business suites, business processes specified with BPEL may be developed at one site and afterwards be executed at other sites without any further transformation. In this manner, business processes spanning organisational boundaries can be specified or modified at a central site and (re)distributed to the enterprises involved for execution in order to serve a common goal.

Such an approach of centralised definition seems to be particularly useful in scenarios where the need of comparatively small modifications of existing local processes to adapt to changing overall requirements occurs frequently and the requirement changes mainly are caused by one of the partners involved. Supply chain management is an example of such a scenario where typically processes of different suppliers have to be coordinated to serve one manufacturer's needs.

In such scenarios, considerable amount of coordination effort could be avoided by central modification and adaptation of the distributed processes. However, concerns that a remotely defined business process could possibly fail to conform to local security policies or, more generally, local business rules often stand in the way of these potential savings. In particular, worry is dedicated to the risk that a business process defined at a site outside the own enterprise and executed on behalf of this external site would fail to obey the restrictions of information and control flows induced by local security policies, may it occur because of insufficient knowledge or because of intentional disregard of such restrictions.

A local process defined as part of an overall process may need access to protected information or resources that, conforming to local security policies, must not be granted to any site outside the own enterprise. Since such local processes typically communicate with other parts of the overall process, such access will only be granted to the local process if it can be made sure that the protected information will not be disclosed across enterprise boundaries and protected resources will only be used within the limits prescribed by security policies.

Checking a process definition for compliance to constraints of information and control flows, ideally prior to execution of the process, is generally considered a demanding task that may easily require more effort than could have been saved by avoiding coordination overhead. This might be the reason why such exploitation of the capability for platform-independent definition of business processes in order to reduce adaptation effort with business processes spanning enterprise boundaries often will not even be envisaged.

In the application layer, security policy enforcement at runtime often is performed by exertion of role-based access control (RBAC). Conforming to the underlying principles of RBAC to safeguard confidentiality and integrity, a business process communicating with sites outside the own enterprise, in general, would not be granted access to protected information or resources. Reason for this is that for the decision to grant access RBAC usually does not take into account the disposition of information provided in the further course of action within the process requesting access. Thus, security policy enforcement at runtime using RBAC offers no alternative to complex analysis of business processes with respect to compliance to security policies prior to execution since RBAC would have to prevent courses of action in enterprise-spanning business processes that are reasonable and required in the context of the overall process.

Hence, we are facing the following dilemma: On one hand side, there is the opportunity to save a considerable amount of effort required for development and adaptation of business processes by exploiting the property of BPEL being a platform-independent standard for the definition of executable business processes. On the other hand side, this opportunity either cannot be made use of because of security concerns or the effort possibly saved has to be spent otherwise for checking compliance to security policies in order to dispel such security concerns.

In this book based on the author's research, methods and procedures will be introduced that help to resolve this dilemma. These procedures allow for performing the required check of compliance to security policies prior to execution of a business process in a comparatively easy way. Even more, the procedures to analyse BPEL scripts defining business processes are suited to be performed automatically such that they can be checked quickly and with little effort. This, of course, is of great value in security policy compliance assessment of remotely-defined business processes in enterprise-spanning scenarios. Furthermore, this approach may also be applied beneficially to save effort in quality assurance when assessing compliance to security policies of business processes that have been developed within an organisation for internal use only.

Finally, the procedures developed for the field of organisation-spanning business processes will be generalised in such a way that they also become applicable with Grid and Cloud computing.

Dr. Klaus-Peter Fischer-Hellmann

June 2012

Vorwort | German Preface

Seit einigen Jahren befindet sich Web Services Business Process Execution Language (WS-BPEL oder kurz BPEL) in weitverbreitetem Einsatz bei der Definition von ausführbaren Geschäftsprozessen. Da es sich bei BPEL um einen Plattformunabhängigen Standard handelt, der von einigen wichtigen Herstellern sogenannter Business Suites unterstützt wird, können Geschäftsprozesse, die mittels BPEL spezifiziert werden, an einem Standort entwickelt und anschließend an anderen Standorten ausgeführt werden, ohne dass dazu weitere Transformationen notwendig sind. Auf diese Weise können Geschäftsprozesse, die organisatorische Grenzen überschreiten, an einer zentralen Stelle spezifiziert oder modifiziert werden und an die beteiligten Unternehmen zur Ausführung übergeben werden, um eine gemeinsame Aufgabe zu erfüllen.

Ein solcher Ansatz einer zentralisierten Definition erscheint besonders dann vorteilhaft, wenn es häufig vorkommt, dass vergleichsweise kleine Änderungen an bestehenden lokalen Prozessen zur Anpassung an geänderte Anforderungen notwendig werden und diese Änderungen hauptsächlich von einem der beteiligten Partner veranlasst sind. Supply Chain Management ist ein Beispiel eines solchen Szenarios, bei dem typischerweise Prozesse verschiedener Lieferanten zu koordinieren sind, um den Bedürfnissen eines Herstellers zu genügen.

In solchen Szenarien kann beträchtlicher Koordinationsaufwand eingespart werden, indem die notwendigen Anpassungen zentral erfolgen. Dem allerdings stehen Bedenken entgegen, dass dabei die lokalen Sicherheitsrichtlinien oder Geschäftsregeln nicht eingehalten werden. Insbesondere gilt die Sorge dem Risiko, dass ein Geschäftsprozess, der außerhalb des eigenen Unternehmens definiert wurde und im Auftrag dieser externen Stelle ausgeführt werden soll, die Beschränkungen des Kontroll- und Informationsflusses nicht beachtet, die sich aus den eigenen Sicherheitsrichtlinien ergeben – sei es aus Unkenntnis oder aufgrund absichtlicher Missachtung derselben.

Ein lokaler Prozess, der Teil eines Gesamtprozesses ist, benötigt möglicherweise Zugriff auf geschützte Informationen oder Ressourcen, der normalerweise einer Stelle außerhalb des eigenen Unternehmens nicht gewährt werden darf. Da solch ein lokaler Prozess typischerweise mit anderen Teilen des Gesamtprozesses kommuniziert, kann ein solcher Zugriff nur gewährt werden, wenn sichergestellt werden kann, dass geschützte Information nicht über die Firmengrenze hinweg verbreitet wird und geschützte Ressourcen nur innerhalb der von den Sicherheitsrichtlinien vorgegebenen Grenzen verwendet werden.

Eine Prozessdefinition auf Einhaltung der Einschränkungen bezüglich Informations- und Kontrollströmen zu überprüfen, idealerweise noch vor deren Ausführung, gilt im Allgemeinen als schwierig und kann sehr schnell einen hohen Aufwand bedeuten. Das könnte der Grund sein, warum an eine solche Ausnutzung der prinzipiell möglichen Plattform-unabhängigen Definition von Geschäftsprozessen zur Reduktion des Anpassungsaufwands bei firmenübergreifenden Geschäftsprozessen häufig nicht einmal gedacht wird.

Auf Anwendungsebene wird die Einhaltung von Sicherheitsrichtlinien zur Laufzeit häufig mit Verfahren gemäß Role-Based Access Control (RBAC) überwacht. Entsprechend den zugrunde liegenden Prinzipien von RBAC zur Sicherstellung von Vertraulichkeit und Integrität dürfte einem Geschäftsprozess, der mit Stellen außerhalb des eigenen Unternehmens kommuniziert, im Allgemeinen kein Zugriff auf geschützte Informationen oder Ressourcen gewährt werden. Dies liegt daran, dass für die Entscheidung, Zugriff zu gewähren, bei RBAC üblicherweise nicht berücksichtigt wird, was im weiteren Verlauf des Prozesses mit der Information geschieht. Daher stellt die Überwachung der Einhaltung von Sicherheitsrichtlinien zur Laufzeit mittels RBAC keine Alternative dar zur komplizierten Analyse eines Geschäftsprozesses vor dessen Ausführung auf Verträglichkeit mit den Sicherheitsrichtlinien, da mit RBAC Abläufe in Firmengrenzen überschreitenden Geschäftsprozessen verboten werden müssten, die jedoch im Sinne des Gesamtprozesses sinnvoll und wünschenswert sind.

Es besteht also folgendes Dilemma: Einerseits besteht die Möglichkeit, beträchtlichen Aufwand bei der Entwicklung und Anpassung von Geschäftsprozessen einzusparen, indem man sich die Eigenschaft von BPEL zunutze macht, ein Plattform-unabhängiger Standard zur Definition ausführbarer Geschäftsprozesse zu sein. Andererseits kann aufgrund von Sicherheitsbedenken von dieser Möglichkeit kein Gebrauch gemacht werden oder der möglicherweise einzusparende Aufwand muss anderweitig wieder investiert werden, um die Vereinbarkeit mit Sicherheitsrichtlinien zu überprüfen, um solche Sicherheitsbedenken zu zerstreuen.

In diesem Buch werden auf den Forschungsarbeiten des Autors basierende Verfahren und Prozeduren vorgestellt, die dazu beitragen, dieses Dilemma zu lösen. Diese Prozeduren ermöglichen es, die notwendige Überprüfung auf Verträglichkeit mit Sicherheitsrichtlinien vor Ausführung eines Geschäftsprozesses auf relativ einfache Weise vorzunehmen. Darüber hinaus eignen sich die Prozeduren zur Analyse von BPEL-Skripten, die Geschäftsprozesse definieren, zur automatischen Durchführung, so dass diese Skripte schnell und mit geringem Aufwand überprüfbar sind. Dies ist natürlich von großem Wert bei der Ermittlung der Verträglichkeit mit Sicherheitsrichtlinien bei an anderer Stelle definierten Geschäftsprozessen in Firmengrenzen überschreitenden Szenarien. Es kann jedoch auch zu verringertem Aufwand bei der Qualitätssicherung beitragen, wenn lokal definierte Geschäftsprozesse, die zur rein internen Verwendung gedacht sind, auf Einhaltung der Sicherheitsrichtlinien zu überprüfen sind.

Schließlich werden die Prozeduren und Verfahren, die für Organisationsgrenzen überschreitende Geschäftsprozesse entwickelt wurden, dahingehend verallgemeinert, dass sie auch für Grid und Cloud Computing einsetzbar werden.

Dr. Klaus-Peter Fischer-Hellmann

Juni 2012

Contents

Lists

List of Figures

List of Tables

List of XML Snippets

Abbreviations and Acronyms

AaaS	Application as a Service
ACM	Association for Computing Machinery
BEA	BEA Systems, Inc.
BPDL	Business Process Definition Language
BPEL	Business Process Execution Language (short form of WS-BPEL)
BPEL4WS	Business Process Execution Language for Web Services (formerly for WS-BPEL)
BPMI.org	Business Process Management Initiative
BSI	Bundesamt für Sicherheit in der Informationstechnik (Federal Agency for Security in Information Technology)
CBP	Cooperative Business Process
CHR	Constraint Handling Rules
CPN	Coloured Petri Net
CTMF	Conformance Testing Methodology and Framework
DAAD	Deutscher Akademischer Austauschdienst
DAC	Discretionary Access Control
DBMS	Data Base Managing System
EFSA	Extended Finite State Automaton (aka Extended Finite State Machine, EFSM)
EM	Event Monitoring
EWSRS	External Web Service Restriction Statement
FQ	Frequency Check of Invocation
GGF	Global Grid Forum
GS	Grid Service
HTTP	Hypertext Transfer Protocol
IaaS	Infrastructure as a Service
IBM	International Business Machines Corp.
IEC	International Electrotechnical Commission
IEEE	Institute of Electrical and Electronics Engineers
IFA	Information Flow Analysis

INESC	Instituto de Engenharia de Sistema e Computadores, Lisbon, Portugal
ISO	International Organization for Standardization
ITU	International Telecommunication Union
IWSRS	Internal Web Service Restriction Statement
MAC	Mandatory Access Control
MLS	Multilevel Security
NIST	National Institute of Standards and Technology
NRG	Network Research Group (University of Plymouth)
OASIS	Organization for the Advancement of Structured Information Standards
OGSA	Open Grid Services Architecture
OGSI	Open Grid Services Infrastructure
OMG	Open Management Group
OrBAC	Organization-Based Access Control
PaaS	Platform as a Service
PCC	Proof Carrying Code
PCV	Policy Consistency Verifier
PDP	Policy Decision Point
PEP	Policy Enforcement Point
RBAC	Role-Based Access Control
RFC	Request for Comment
SAC	Security Assessment Centre
SAML	Security Assertion Markup Language
SAP	SAP AG
SLA	Service Level Agreement
SOA	Service-Oriented Architecture
SOAP	Simple Object Access Protocol
SOC	Service-Oriented Computing
SoD	Separation of Duty
SPS	Security Policy Statement
UDDI	Universal Description, Discovery, and Integration
UML	Unified Modeling Language
UN	United Nations

UN/CEFACT	United Nations Centre for Trade Facilitation and Electronic Business
URI	Universal Resource Identifier
VO	Virtual Organisation
W3C	World Wide Web Consortium
WFMS	Workflow Management System
WS	Web Service
WSCI	Web Services Choreography Interface
WSDL	Web Services Description Language
WS-BPEL	Web Services Business Process Execution Language (abbr. BPEL)
XACML	eXtensible Access Control Markup Language
XML	eXtensible Markup Language
XPath	XML Path Language
XPDL	XML Process Definition Language
XQuery	XML Query Language
XSLT	Extensible Stylesheet Language Transformation

1 Introduction

Service-oriented architecture (SOA) and service-oriented computing (SOC) are currently considered to be the most promising paradigms for distributed computing[1]. A significant amount of research has been dedicated to this field[2] and also standardisation organisation such as OASIS[3] and The Open Group have provided appropriate definitions and a set of standards and recommendations for SOA[4]. Web services and the composition or choreography and orchestration of them play a central role in approaches to service oriented computing[5]. Service orientation is also expected to have an important influence in the field of Grid computing and Cloud computing, where the provisioning of computing resources within a conceptual huge network of collaborating computers and devices can also be fostered by services (so-called Grid services[6] in Grid contexts) provided by different nodes[7].

In service-oriented approaches using Web services, a layered architecture for composing new services from existing services or for executing processes based on existing services has emerged[8], as shown in Figure 1[9]. The communication aspects reside in the bottom layer. Messages between Web services and other communication partners are exchanged using standardised protocols such as SOAP[10] and HTTP[11]. The layer above, the content layer, contains the definition of Web services, thereby providing an SOA in order to allow for service-oriented computing. Web Services Description Language (WSDL)[12] is used for the definition of Web services in this layer while Universal Description, Discovery and Integration (UDDI)[13] is intended for publication and discovery of Web services provided by an organisation in order to be used by others.

---

1 Curbera *et al.*, 2003; Foster and Tuecke, 2005; Papazoglou and Georgakopoulos, 2003
2 *e.g.*, Deubler *et al.*, 2004; Papazoglou and Van den Heuvel, 2007; Deng *et al.*, 2008; Esfahani *et. al.*, 2011
3 Organization for the Advancement of Structured Information Standards
4 *e.g.*, MacKenzie *et al.*, 2006; The Open Group, 2011
5 Berardi *et al.*, 2003
6 Tuecke *et al.*, 2003
7 Höing, 2010; Tai, 2011
8 Medjahed *et al.*, 2003
9 adapted from *ibid.*, p.56
10 Box *et al.*, 2000
11 Fielding *et al.*, 1999
12 Chinnici *et al.*, 2007; Christensen *et al.*, 2001
13 Clement *et al.*, 2004

Business Process Layer	Vendor-Specific or Standardized Business Process Definition Technology
Content Layer	Web Services, WSDL $\rightarrow$ SOA, SOC
Communication Layer	SOAP, HTTP

Figure 1: Layered Architecture in Business-to-Business Interaction

While Web services are stateless by their definition, stateful processes reside in the top layer of this architecture, defining potentially long running business processes based on the invocation of Web services. Business process definition languages (BPDLs) are used for the purpose of defining the orchestration and choreography of Web services in order to establish a business process. It should be noted that a business process defined using one of these languages can itself be considered a Web service from the point of view of external communication parties.

The request for fast adaptation of enhanced services and business processes to changing requirements led to a framework denoted as business process management. Methods for the specification of business processes in the top-most layer of Figure 1 play a central role. For this purpose, a high-level definition language is used abstracting from as many aspects as possible covered in the layers below. After an initial period where vendor-specific definition languages have been used coming with platforms for specification and execution of business processes, the need of standardisation to avoid dependency on certain platforms (vendor lock-in) has grown leading to a variety of business process definition languages (BPDLs) for the specification of enhanced Web services or business processes in the top layer of Figure 1. These BPDLs were initiated by different standardisation organisations or vendor groups. Of course, having competing standards aiming the same purpose detracts from the very function of seeking for standardisation in a particular field. Fortunately, one among these standard propositions, namely Web Services Business Process Execution Language (WS-BPEL or BPEL for short) propagated by the Organization for the Advancement of Structured Information Standards (OASIS) backed by many prominent vendors of business application platforms, evolved the de facto standard in this field[14] even prior to its official acceptance as an OASIS standard in April 2007[15]. In addition, several business suites from major vendors directly support execution of business processes defined in BPEL without the need to first convert BPEL scripts into bytecode or machine code (*e.g.*, IBM

---

14 *e.g.*, Pu *et al.*, 2006; Ouyang *et al.*, 2009
15 OASIS, 2007

WebSphere[16] and Oracle SOA Suite[17]). Hence, BPEL can be considered the BPDL of choice for specifying *executable* business processes.

Based on methods for platform-independent definition of business processes offered by such standardisation, the growing demand for specification of cross-organisational business processes was fostered. Collaborative business processes (CBPs) came to the centre of interest of some research[18]. With CBPs, the specification of the interoperability aspects between different organisations is important while the organisation-specific aspects how a particular functionality or a service is provided could remain opaque. However, specifying a CBP at one location and distributing the specifications to the partner organisations involved in such a CBP for execution could be another approach. This approach is essentially fostered by the use of standardised specification languages for business processes.

1.1   Aims and Objectives

Since security already is an important issue in distributed applications in general, this topic is also of significant importance for CBPs and, in particular, for the application of BPDLs. Security of Web services is well studied and several approaches for access control to Web services exist[19]. Role-based access control (RBAC)[20] is the widely used concept for dealing with security aspects in this field. However, novel security aspects not covered in the aforementioned approaches arise from the distributed definition and execution of CBPs. The following questions have to be answered in this context:

- Are the semantics of a remotely defined business process compatible with the security policy effective at the node where it is to be executed?
- Which classification, with respect to access control, is required for the Web service offered by the remotely defined business process in order to be compliant with the security policy in the domain where it will be executed?

It is anticipated that becoming able to cope with security issues arising from distributed definition and execution of business processes using standardised BPDLs such as BPEL[21] will foster the acceptance of cross-organisational development of business processes (*i.e.*, specification of BPDL scripts remotely from the site of execution). This may allow additional capabilities provided by these standards to be deployed in practical applications such as supply chain management. Since the

---

16 Iyengar *et al.*, 2007
17 Jellema and Dikmans, 2010
18 *e.g.*, Lippe *et al.* 2005; Coetzee and Eloff, 2003; Roser *et al.*, 2011
19 *e.g.*, Abendroth and Jensen, 2003; Dimmock *et al.*, 2004; BSI, 2009
20 Ferraiolo and Kuhn, 1992; Ferraiolo *et al.*, 2001; Peng and Chen, 2004; Hummer *et al.*, 2011
21 Alves *et al.*, 2007

second of the above questions is already in the scope of other related work, the methods and procedures presented in this book are aimed to address the first question.

To this extent, the following objectives have been established from the outset that should be fulfilled by the results achieved:

1) Analysis of the security-relevant semantics of BPDL-defined business processes, in particular in environments where the BPDL scripts specifying a business process are being defined remotely from the location of execution.

2) Based on the results of this analysis, development of a framework for assessing compliance of remotely defined business processes with security policies effective at the location of their execution. This includes a method for defining security policies in terms of security-relevant semantics of BPDLs in order to facilitate the assessment process.

3) Development of methods for compliance assessment preferably based on technologies customary in the context of SOA established on Web services and business processes. The reason for this objective is to aim at ease of applicability for practitioners accustomed to the specification of Web services and business processes. In order to apply the methods proposed in this book, potential users should not be forced to acquire additional skills in addition to those already acquainted in the field of application.

4) Investigation of the methods proposed with respect to their suitability for automatic performance of compliance assessment. Being able to perform compliance assessment with as little as possible human intervention was deemed to support acceptance of such methods.

5) Evaluation of the feasibility of the framework for practical applications by prototypically implementing parts of it and evaluating this prototype in a test bed environment.

Note:

Throughout the book, the term *security policy* is understood to comprise all kinds of rules that may imply access restrictions to information or resources or may impose boundaries for information and control flows independent of the reason for this limitation. Some of such rules belonging to security policies with this notion might not be considered security rules by other authors, but would rather be identified as business rules. All such rules are uniformly denoted *security rules* herein because assessment of compliance to any of these rules can be checked independently of the motivation that led to the rule. How to perform the required checks for such assessment only depends on the kind of restriction caused by the respective rule. A collection of security rules constitutes a *security policy*.

It should be noted that even though the methods developed based on the above objectives for compliance assessment of BPDL-defined business processes have been motivated by the situation of cooperative business processes distributed across enterprise boundaries, they can also be advantageously applied in strictly local environments where development and execution of business processes are performed within a single organisation. Also without remote specification of business processes, effort for assessing compliance to local security policies in the course of quality assurance procedures may be reduced considerably if the capability of automatic performance required by Objective 4 in the list above is exploited.

1.2   Structure of this Book

In Chapter 2, the current use of business process definition languages and conceivable extensions of its application, in particular in the context of CBPs, are discussed. Using a comprehensive example of a distributed business process taken from the context of supply chain management, which will be used throughout the book, security issues arising in the field of Web services and business processes are considered, in particular in situations where definition and execution of business processes are distributed across security domain boundaries.

The state of the art of specifying and enforcing security policies in general, as well as in SOA-based applications and in application environments using mobile code, in particular with respect to access control and information flow control, is discussed in Chapter 3. In addition, restricting the scope on a particular representative of BPDLs, namely WS-BPEL, is justified in this section.

Chapter 4 contains an overview of WS-BPEL as a specification language and presents the results from the analysis of the security-relevant semantics of WS-BPEL. To this extent, security policy-induced restrictions for Web service invocations have been classified and so-called security-relevant semantic patterns have been derived from this classification.

In Chapter 5, the results of this analysis are applied to propose a method for the specification of security policies that helps to facilitate the process of security policy assessment for cross-organisationally defined business processes. In addition, approaches to reduce the complexity of security policy specifications and to cope with dynamic aspects in pre-execution security policy assessment are discussed.

Chapter 6 takes a deeper look into the process of assessing the security-relevant behaviour by inspecting WS-BPEL scripts in order to determine the compliance to security policies and introduces an architecture that allows for separation of the security analysis and assessment of WS-BPEL scripts and the displacement of these tasks to special nodes in an application environment.

In Chapter 7, the prototype specified and implemented as proof of concept will be presented. After introducing the scope of the prototypical implementation, the method of specifying security policy statements introduced in Chapter 5 in a machine-processible manner will be explained. Furthermore, the architecture of the prototype, the hierarchy of Java classes and the algorithms used for assessment of compliance with security policies and, in particular, for information flow analysis will be discussed. The chapter sums up the results of the proof of concept by presenting the evaluation of the prototype.

Chapter 8 is concerned with possible extensions to methods presented here for business processes in order to allow for a wider applicability. Actually, the transfer of the results to the field of Grid computing and Cloud computing is discussed. The extent to which such transfer is possible is demonstrated, and issues for further research instigated by this approach are identified.

Finally, Chapter 9 contains a summary of and conclusions drawn from the contributions presented herein, and discusses limitations and directions for further research based on these results.

Readers who only want to get an overview of the methods and procedures introduced in this book may browse Chapter 2 to get a deeper look at the problem field and a glimpse of the example from supply chain management used throughout the book, but may skip Chapters 3 and 7, in the first instance. However, the classification contained in Section 3.6 will be required to understand the conclusions drawn in Section 9.1, but reading this section may be postponed until reaching Chapter 9. The main contributions of the book will be derived and presented in Chapters 4 and 5 while Chapter 6 discusses different aspects of applying these contributions in practice. After browsing Chapter 2, readers mainly interested in the extensions to the field of Grid computing and Cloud computing should at least read Chapters 4 and 5 before skipping to Chapter 8. Chapter 7 contains a comprehensive overview of the prototype implementing the procedures for compliance assessment introduced in Chapter 5. Therefore, Chapter 7 is recommended to readers who want to get an impression as to how automatic performance of compliance assessment based on the methods and procedures developed in Chapters 4 through 6 could be implemented.

2 Cross-Organisational Deployment of Business Processes

In this chapter, we take a deeper look at the problem area and provide a comprehensive example from the field of supply chain management that will be used throughout the book, particularly in Chapters 4, 5, and 7, to explicate various aspects of the approaches introduced herein. Readers interested in an overview of the results presented may browse this chapter to only get an impression of the problems motivating the methods and procedures described in this book and to get an idea of the running example also used in other chapters.

Collaborative business processes (CBPs) as defined, for instance, by Coetzee and Eloff[22] denote business processes that span organisational boundaries in order to support business interactions involving cross-organisational workflows. Modelling of such CBPs has been discussed, for instance, by Lippe *et. al.*[23]. The definition of workflow views that provide as much information as required to allow for specification of CBPs assuring cross-organisational interoperability, but at the same time as less information as possible about the internal aspects of a workflow as implemented by a particular partner in a CBP is considered essential[24]. Approaches to provide the required functionality for cross-organisational workflows based on SOA are considered particularly beneficial[25]. SOC established by those approaches facilitates the definition of CBPs. Standardised BPDLs play a central role in the definition of CBPs due to their ability to specify business processes on top of Web services and their platform-independency[26]. Though currently the definition of executable business processes across organisational boundaries seems not yet to have found much interest in research, using standardised BPDLs particularly for this purpose would exploit the capability offered by a standard more than is done currently. This consideration will be explained in more detail below.

In an SOC environment, first the situation is considered where the task of defining CBPs and related enhanced Web services using a BPDL is distributed between several nodes in different organisations. This state-of-the-art employment of a BPDL, where each organisation engaged in a particular CBP defines on its own the respective business processes or enhanced Web services executed within their system, is

---

22 Coetzee and Eloff, 2003
23 Lippe *et. al.*, 2006
24 Dickson *et al.*, 2004
25 Papazoglou and van den Heuvel, 2007
26 Sayaha and Zhang, 2005

depicted in Figure 2. Of course, agreement on the overall task of the CBP has to be achieved between the organisations involved.

Figure 2 illustrates an exemplary environment for the distributed development and execution of a BPDL-defined collaborative business process, with two systems residing in two different domains A and B. Each node depicted in Figure 2 is supposed to belong to a different organisation, but still is capable of running processes defined in a particular BPDL.

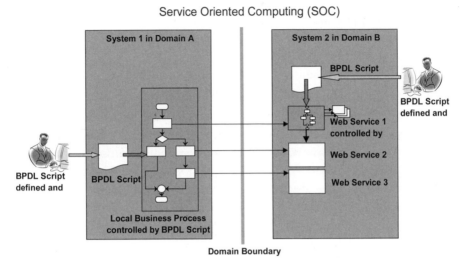

Figure 2: Collaborative Business Process Using Locally Defined Subprocesses

Consider the case where in domain A there is a need for a CBP, for instance, in a supply chain application, requiring information I_A offered by a Web service W_2 at system 2 in domain B. Because of restrictions imposed by security policies in domain B, Web service W_2 would not be allowed to be accessed directly from outside domain B, because, for instance, it provides further information besides I_A that must not be leaked from domain B. For solving this conflict with security policy restrictions, a conventional approach would be the provision of an enhanced Web service in domain B, say W_1 at system 2. W_1 would access the information required from Web service W_2 and offer the non-restricted part of the results (*i.e.*, I_A) to system 1 in domain A across the domain boundary. Since a business process defined by a BPDL script offers services to its environment, it can itself be considered a Web service. Therefore, in this example W_1 is assumed to be defined by a BPDL script S_1.

2.1 Extended Use of Business Process Definition Languages in CBP Scenarios

In order to allow for fast development and adaptation to changing requirements of business processes, it would be desirable to concentrate the definition of all business processes and enhanced Web services at one particular node and distribute the BPDL script resulting from this location to other nodes for execution. This would reduce the coordination overhead implied by distributed definition of the parts of the CBP in different organisations and, therefore, could help to save time and to increase flexibility during the specification and implementation of CBPs.

Since the need for the particular business process in this example arose in domain A, it is very probable that also requests for changes to this business process will arise in this domain. In order to circumvent the requirement that requests for change arising in domain A must be presented to developers in domain B in order to have them change the Web service W_1, it would be conceivable that W_1 running on behalf of a business process in domain A will be defined by developers in domain A. The defining BPDL script S_1 will subsequently be brought to execution at system 2 in domain B as indicated by the arc from the developer workstation at domain A to domain B in Figure 3.

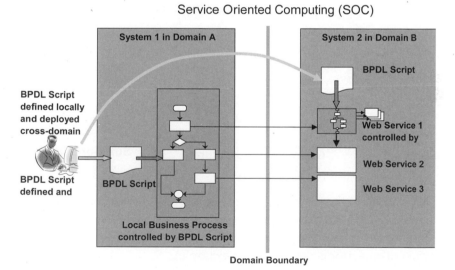

Figure 3: Cross-Organisational Deployment of Business Processes

This approach would greatly facilitate the adaptation of W_1 in domain B to changing requirements originating in domain A. Given both systems are based on a BPDL-enabled platform using the same preferably standardised BPDL, this scenario, as depicted in Figure 3, would be technically feasible. However, it would induce severe security weaknesses in domain B, if S_1 would be executed in domain B without particular precautions. Prior to running S_1, it has to be determined whether the semantics of W_1 defined by S_1 comply with security policies effective in domain B. Unless these security issues can be solved, it may prevent this extended use of BPDL scripts from being actually applied in a real-world cross-organisational environment.

2.2 Motivating Example of Cross-Organisational Business Process

In Figure 4, an example from the area of supply chain management (SCM) is shown that will be used to illustrate the security issues arising when remotely defined BPDL scripts are being deployed across enterprise domain boundaries.

Supply Chain Management

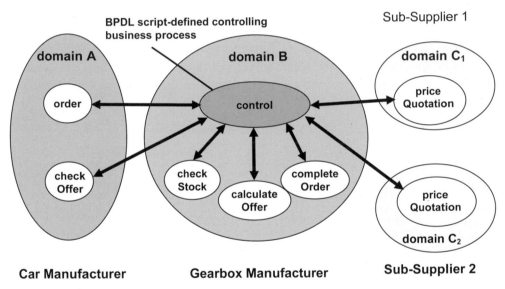

Figure 4: Collaborative Business Process Example

The application context of the distributed business process depicted in Figure 4 is the order processing of a car manufacturer ordering gearboxes or components thereof from a gearbox manufacturer who, in turn, orders components for gearboxes from different sub-suppliers (two in this example).

The business process is set up in a SOC environment where all functions used for the application are provided as Web services and the composition of Web services is accomplished using BPDL for the definition of the controlling workflow. In such a context, BPDL scripts are not required to perform any kind of data manipulation or data processing. Since standardised BPDLs usually do not provide any language constructs for performing data manipulations, constructs of other languages such as XQuery[27], XSLT[28], and XPath[29] would have to be imported for these purposes. Since in a service oriented application context, all data processing can be kept outside the controlling BPDL scripts, it is assumed that the BPDL scripts considered here only make use of elements imported from XPath, if any, in expressions specifying conditions for flow control purposes not implying any data manipulation.

2.2.1 Description of Business Process Example

In this example, a BPDL script is executed in a system of the gearbox manufacturer defining a controlling business process denoted by `control` in Figure 4. An `order` process of the car manufacturer (that may itself be a Web service or a BPDL-defined business process) invokes the Web service offered by the `control` process at the gearbox manufacturer providing a list of gearbox components to be ordered by the car manufacturer. Before placing an order, the car manufacturer expects a price offer accompanied by a commitment with respect to the delivery date.

The `control` process invokes a `checkStock` Web service for checking the availability of the ordered items in stock. For this purpose, the list of items to be ordered is passed to this Web service. After checking the availability in stock, the `check-Stock` Web service returns two lists of items that are to be ordered from sub-supplier 1 and sub-supplier 2, respectively. Together with these lists of items, a transaction ID for the order in progress and the credentials required to invoke the respective Web services of the two sub-suppliers are returned by `checkStock`.

Upon receiving the response of `checkStock`, the `control` process invokes the `priceQuotation` Web services of the sub-suppliers and provides the respective list of items to each of them. In order to get access to these Web services, the credentials returned by `checkStock` are used by the `control` process. Of course, each Web service of the two sub-suppliers requires its own set of credentials. Therefore, the `control` process has to provide the proper instance of credentials to each of them.

After checking availability of the items on the respective list, each `priceQuotation` Web service returns a list augmented by prices and availability on stock or dates of delivery. The `control` process then invokes a `calculateOffer` Web service of the gearbox manufacturer to prepare an offer for the car manufacturer. For this purpose, the `control` process passes the augmented lists returned from both sub-suppliers to the `calculateOffer` Web service together with the transaction ID that was returned to it before by the `checkStock` Web service.

The `calculateOffer` Web service uses the transaction ID to identify the proper order request of the car manufacturer and to find the information relating to this

27 Boag *et al.*, 2007
28 Kay, 2007
29 Berglund *et al.*, 2006

order in the data base of the gearbox manufacturer provided there by the `check-Stock` Web service. For instance, information about items found to be available in stock and potentially reserved for this order by the `checkStock` Web service could be identified by the `calculateOffer` Web service in the course of its processing. Finally, the offer is returned to the `control` process and will be passed to a `check-Offer` Web service of the car manufacturer. This Web service will return an 'OK' or 'Reject' response to the `control` process after having checked whether the offer would be acceptable to the car manufacturer.

The response from the `checkOffer` Web service is passed to a `completeOrder` Web service by the `control` process. Depending on the type of response, this Web service either completes the order processing within the gearbox manufacturer if the response was 'OK' or discards all intermediate information such as items reserved for this transaction ID if the response was 'Reject'.

After the `completeOrder` Web service has terminated its task, it returns a corresponding result to the `control` process that, in turn, provides this result to the `order` Web service of the car manufacturer as a response to its own invocation, thereby completing the workflow of this business process.

For the purpose of this discussion it is supposed that the `control` process could be specified by the car manufacturer as a BPDL script and sent to the gearbox manufacturer for execution within his domain. Reasons for doing so could be the ability to better adapt the order processing with respect to the communication requirements between the car manufacturer and the gearbox manufacturer, and to react faster to changing requests concerning the workflow on the side of the car manufacturer, thereby providing more flexibility for definition of the collaborative business process to the car manufacturer. However, unless the security issues related with this approach (as discussed in the next section) could be solved satisfactorily, the gearbox manufacturer would not accept this remotely defined BPDL script for execution.

2.2.2 Security Policy-Induced Restrictions in Cross-Organisational Business Process Execution

When the controlling BPDL script is brought in from the car manufacturer for execution in the domain of the gearbox manufacturer, the processing performed by the controlling business process will be subject to several restrictions derived from security policies of the gearbox manufacturer.

The security policies of the gearbox manufacturer may mandate that the list of items that are not in stock and, therefore, have to be ordered from the sub-suppliers may not be disclosed to the car manufacturer and the respective competing sub-supplier for strategic reasons. The same will obviously hold for the credentials required for granting access to the `priceQuotation` Web services of the sub-suppliers. This information may only be passed to the respective sub-supplier, but neither to the competing sub-supplier nor to the car manufacturer for obvious security reasons.

Other restrictions in the example of Figure 4 may require that the list containing prices and delivery dates for the items to be ordered returned by each of the sub-suppliers has to be passed unmodified to the `calculateOffer` Web service while the respective source of the lists may not be confused in order to allow for proper calculation of an offer to the car manufacturer. Finally, this information may also not be disclosed to the car manufacturer or the competing sub-supplier. Furthermore, it may be required that the offer containing prices and delivery dates returned from the `calculateOffer` Web service is passed to the `checkOffer` Web service of the car manufacturer without any modification in order to prevent manipulation of this offer, for instance, by changing the committed delivery date or the prices.

A further type of possible restrictions implied by security policies of the gearbox manufacturer may require that particular input parameters of a Web service may not be used, or only be used with a restricted range of allowed values if invoked in a BPDL script imported from the car manufacturer. An example of such restrictions could be the `calculateOffer` Web service that could have a further input parameter for controlling the type of rebate to be taken into account in calculating the offer. If invoked by the `control` process defined by the car manufacturer, this parameter may be forbidden to be used at all of may be restricted to one or a few values. Without such a restriction, the car manufacturer could define in the `control` process any amount of rebate the `calculateOffer` Web service is able to provide, even though the gearbox manufacturer usually would only allow a specific amount of discount to this car manufacturer.

2.3 Security Issues Related to Cross-Organisational Deployment of CBP

As can be seen from the foregoing discussion, many restrictions refer to non-disclosure of information passed between Web services within the `control` process to destinations outside the domain of the gearbox manufacturer, in particular to the car manufacturer. The latter restriction is of special interest facing the fact that in the example above this very process is defined by exactly the car manufacturer who is restricted to get some of the information handled by this process.

Other restrictions mandate that the values passed to a Web service originate from a particular other Web service or lie in a particular range of values.

Access control to Web services[30] and in particular role-based access control (RBAC)[31] may only cover part of these restrictions. If addressed by access control

---

30 *e.g.* Abendroth and Jensen, 2003; Dimmock *et al.*, 2004

means alone, enforcement of non-disclosure of information outside the local domain would imply that access to the particular information would not be granted to any principal outside the local domain. In this example, the car manufacturer residing outside the local domain of the gearbox manufacturer and, as a consequence, also the BPDL script defined and invoked by the car manufacturer, would not be granted access to visibility restricted information thus preventing the `control` process of this example being remotely defined and deployed by the car manufacturer.

Relaxation of access restrictions, such as granting access provided the values passed to a Web service come from a particular source (for instance values returned from a specific Web service), require information flow (in backwards direction) to be considered for making decisions upon granting access or not. Thus, information flow analysis has to be applied in addition to purely access control-oriented approaches, in order to cope with this kind of restrictions.

Restrictions with respect to visibility of values returned from a Web service are also not covered by access control measures alone. For this purpose, information flow (in forward direction) has to be analysed, that means the future use of the values returned has to be taken into consideration.

With the approach proposed here, these restrictions derived from the security policies at the location where a remotely defined BPDL script will be executed can be enforced using the methods proposed, including the restriction that the author of the BPDL script is precluded from getting knowledge about information handled by the business process he has specified. At first sight, the last one may seem to be a restriction contradictory to itself. However, it will turn out during the course of further consideration that it is possible to grant access in such a fine-grained manner to a remotely defined business process and enforce the implied information flow restrictions in a straightforward manner at the executing site.

The security issues arising when remotely defined BPDL scripts are to be executed can be condensed into the following questions:

1) Will the business process defined by the BPDL script comply with the security policies of the executing domain?

2) Which access privileges are required in order to grant access to the business process defined by the BPDL script (*i.e.*, to possess the proper privileges for accessing the resources, particularly the Web services, encountered in the course of its execution)?

The second question is addressed by research considering access control[32], even though not necessarily in the context of BPDL script execution[33]. The first question,

---

31 Ferraiolo *et al.*, 2001; Peng and Chen, 2004
32 Koshutanski and Massacci, 2003; Mendling *et al.*, 2004

however, is comparatively novel since execution of remotely defined BPDL scripts seems currently not to be in practical use very much and, therefore, security aspects inherent in this way of using BPDL have not found a lot of attention in research, yet.

The research leading to the results presented in the following chapters has strived to propose a framework for coping with these novel security aspects arising from the employment of standardised business process languages. To this end, semantic aspects of the business processes defined by their respective scripts written, for instance, in BPDL, are considered at the time, a new script is to be deployed to a node across security boundaries. However, the analysis of the semantics of code written in programming languages is a well-known difficulty[34]. Therefore, the need to analyse the semantics of a BPDL-defined business process with respect to involved security-relevant semantics would make the approach to specify a business process remotely from the location of execution impractical unless this analysis can be provided automatically, at least to a large extent. The methodology proposed will make use of the fact, that business process languages offer little to none means for defining data processing or computational tasks as part of the language itself, but rather have to invoke Web services for these purposes or must import constructs from expression languages defined in other XML standards such as XSLT[35], XQuery[36], or XPath[37].

The extended use of business processes as proposed in Section 2.1 and parts of the framework for assessing compliance of remotely defined BPDL scripts described in chapters 4 through 6 have been published in several workshop, conference, and journal papers[38].

2.4 Limitation of Scope to WS-BPEL without Loss of Generality

For the definition of Web services, Web Services Description Language (WSDL) 1.1[39] (expected to be gradually substituted by its newer version WSDL 2.0[40]) has been established by the World Wide Web Consortium (W3C) as a single standard broadly accepted for the definition of Web services.

---

33 Joshi *et al.*, 2001
34 Cousot 1999
35 Kay, 2007
36 Boag *et al.*, 2007
37 Berglund *et al.*, 2006
38 Fischer *et al.*, 2005, Fischer *et al.*, 2006, Fischer *et al.*, 2007a, Fischer *et al.*, 2007b, Fischer *et al.*, 2007c
39 Christensen *et al.*, 2001
40 Chinnici *et al.*, 2007

In contrast, for business process definition languages (BPDLs) several approaches to standardisation have been taken by different vendor groups and standardisation organisations, leading to a plurality of standards:

- Web Services Business Process Execution Language (WS-BPEL), formerly known as Business Process Execution Language for Web Services (BPEL4WS or BPEL for short)[41], propagated by the Organisation for the Advancement of Structured Information Standards (OASIS),
- Business Process Modelling Language (BPML)[42], propagated by the Business Process Management Initiative (BPMI.org); since merger between BPMI.org and Object Management Group (OMG) in 2005, standardisation activities for BPML has been dropped in favour of BPEL,
- XML Process Definition Language (XPDL)[43], propagated by the Workflow Management Coalition,
- Web Services Choreography Interface (WSCI)[44], propagated by the World Wide Web Consortium (W3C),
- ebXML Business Process Specification Schema[45], propagated by UN/CEFACT and OASIS, and
- Business Process Model And Notation (BPMN), Version 2.0[46], initially propagated by BPMI.org; after merger with OMG in 2005, BPMN is supported and has been standardised as Version 2.0 by OMG.

Though the existence of several parallel standards aiming at the same goal, in general, adversely affect the very purpose of standardisation, the different standards at least have some obvious commonalities, as all languages except of BPMN are script-based using XML[47] and facilitate the composition of business processes by invocation of Web services and definition of the communication with other parties (in particular human participants) involved in a business process.

Among these standards, BPMN plays a special role since it provides a graphical notation for representing business processes to be specified and may be best compared with UML as a modelling tool. Being a graph-based notation for business processes, BPMN is considered better suited for business analysts. However, using it without special tools to draw the graphic required seems to be very complicated and could be considered nearly impossible. Further, in order to become executable, BPMN-based process specifications need to be mapped to another representation such as XPDL or BPEL. The BPMN standard comprises a mapping to BPEL, al-

41 Alves *et al.*, 2007
42 Arkin, 2002
43 Workflow Management Coalition, 2008
44 Arkin *et al.*, 2002
45 Dubray *et al.*, 2006
46 OMG, 2011
47 Bray *et al.*, 2006

though it has been argued that not all process modelling supported by BPMN can be mapped to BPEL. For this reason, some people particularly in favour of BPMN argue that BPMN is to be considered superior to BPEL[48]. In spite of these arguments, many authors still rate BPEL as the de facto standard for defining business processes, at least, executable ones[49].

The fact that several business process languages exist in parallel, gave rise to research as to which extent these languages are comparable with respect to their semantic expressiveness[50]. In particular, Aalst *et al.*[51] and Wohed *et al.*[52] analysed different languages (*i.e.*, WS-BPEL, BPML, WSCI and some vendor-specific business process languages) with respect to workflow and communication patterns. The results of their work indicate that, to a large extent, the different languages are capable of expressing the same semantics with respect to workflow control and communication behaviour.

As was to be expected from these results, the different languages may be convertible to each other as has been shown in an exemplary manner for XPDL and WS-BPEL by Fischer and Wenzel[53].

In other work[54], a process ontology based on multiple meta-models derived from different existing workflow models is introduced in order to facilitate mappings between choreography descriptions defining possible interactions between different partners of a CBP and internal workflows of the partners defined using different workflow languages, workflow models, and choreography languages. One successful mapping (with manual intervention) between a vendor-specific workflow definition language and Abstract BPEL (specification of abstract, *i.e.*, not executable, business processes defined in BPEL) is reported. Although successful automatic conversion between different workflow definition languages and BPDLs based on their proposition does not seem to have been published ever since, this approach and the preliminary results reported so far underpin the assumption that mapping between different workflow definition languages and different BPDLs is possible and conversion of business process specifications based on a particular BPDL may be converted into a semantically equivalent specification based on another BPDL. In addition, this conversion has been shown to be performed automatically, at least up to a certain extent.

Given the fundamental similarity of all different languages used for business process definition and their potential to be converted to each other, the scope of novel

---

48   Vigneras, 2008; Swenson, 2008
49   *e.g.*, Ouyang *et al.*, 2009, Merouani *et al.*, 2010
50   Aalst *et al.*, 2002; Shapiro, 2002; Wohed *et al.*, 2002
51   Aalst *et al.*, 2002
52   Wohed *et al.*, 2002
53   Fischer and Wenzel, 2004
54   Haller *et al.*, 2006; Haller and Oren, 2006

methods presented here has been focussed on one particular representative, namely WS-BPEL. In 2007, WS-BPEL has been accepted by the Organization for the Advancement of Structured Information Standards (OASIS) as an OASIS standard[55]. Prior to this, through support by prominent vendors like IBM, Oracle, BEA, Microsoft, SAP, and Siebel, WS-BPEL already had emerged as the de-facto standard for business process definition[56].

According to common practice, for the remainder of the book BPEL will be used as a short-hand for WS-BPEL.

2.5 Summary

In this section, the main goal of the research that led to the results presented in the following chapters, namely the assessment of compliance of remotely defined BPEL scripts with local security policy, has been motivated by discussing some of the security issues arising by executing remotely defined BPEL scripts. A comprehensive example from the field of supply chain management has been introduced for this purpose, which will also be used in other chapters for explication of various aspects of the approaches presented. The example has shown that availability of fine-grained access control and information flow control may enable sensible tasks to be performed by remotely defined business processes without jeopardising local security policy.

Since the different standardised BPDLs are comparable with respect to their expressiveness for specifying the process logic of a business process and BPEL is considered the de-facto standard for specification of executable business process as underpinned by related work discussed above, without loss of generality, the scope of consideration will be restricted to BPEL in the remainder of the book.

---

55 OASIS, 2007
56 Wang *et al.*, 2004; Mayer and Lübcke, 2006

3 Approaches to Specification and Enforcement of Security Policies

In SOA-Security-Kompendium [57], a variety of security aspects to be observed with SOA based on Web services and ways to cope with them is described. Approaches to cope with security policy enforcement in general, and of Web services and business processes, in particular, being only part of what is contained there, will be discussed in this chapter. Possible methods include validation (or even verification) prior to execution, or by monitoring and intervening during execution of a program. In addition, because a BPEL-defined business process can itself be considered a Web service, approaches to specify security requirements of Web services and to solve security issues with Web services may also relate to business processes defined this way and, therefore, will be considered in this chapter, too.

Readers mainly interested in the novel approaches introduced in this book may skip this chapter in the first instance, but should come back, at least, to read Section 3.6 prior to reading the conclusions in Chapter 9. However, readers not acquainted with the notion of covert channels should have a look at the explanation on page 28 or at the example in Section 6.1.4 prior to proceeding to Chapter 4.

Since from the outset, the scope was particularly focussed on scenarios where BPEL scripts are defined at one location and brought to a remote location for execution, approaches to solve security issues arising with execution of mobile code are also considered. This is because the distributed definition and execution scenario for BPEL scripts is, to a large extent, similar to the situation where mobile code is to be executed. Common to both situations is the fact that from the point of view of the executing site, the script or code, respectively, has been defined remotely and is brought in for execution on an ad-hoc basis such as applets contained in a Web page and downloaded via HTTP together with the page content.

As a consequence thereof, it is not clear at first sight what this script or code is going to do when executed; that is, the semantics of the script or code are unknown (at least the details thereof while the overall semantics, *e.g.*, collecting information for an order in a B2B application) may be known. Because of this, among others, there may be concerns about the possible effects to the local system environment resulting from its execution. In particular, there will be concerns as to whether the script or code will obey security policies effective at the domain executing it.

Unlike other scenarios of executing remotely defined code (such as executing programs developed and installed by the IT department of one's own organisations or

---

57 BSI, 2009

programs being part of a product supplied by a well-known vendor), when executing mobile code there is not usually a level of trust that is appropriate to alleviate the concerns about the potential of the remotely defined program to cause harm to the local environment or to violate the local security policies. However, even with programs developed or installed by the organisation's IT department, trustworthiness may be arguable because of potential infection of this software with malicious code injected during Internet communication. This general and apparently increasing risk of getting infected by viruses, Trojan horses or spyware[58] gives rise to employ anti-virus and anti-spyware check software. However, this risk of malicious modification after deployment is not typical to BPEL scripts and may be prohibited by appropriate mechanisms of the platform executing such scripts. Consequently, since this risk and possible countermeasures are neither novel nor specific in the scenario considered in this book, these will be considered out of scope.

If developed remotely from the executing site, but still within the same organisational domain, domain-internal regulations such as quality assurance procedures applied during the development process could help to assess a program or script as conforming to security policies of the security domain in which the program is to run. After such assessment, a program can by considered trusted code. But this does not apply in situations that are of particular interest in the scope of this book. Therefore, security concerns with respect to cross-organisational deployment of BPEL scripts can be best compared with security concerns that exist if untrusted, remotely defined code is to be executed. Therefore, approaches to solving security issues with the execution of mobile code may also be applicable to, or at least may serve as a model for approaches to solve the comparable issues with cross-organisational deployment of BPEL scripts. An overview of conventional approaches to cope with security issues involved in the execution of mobile code is given by Rubin and Geer[59].

3.1   Specification of Security Aspects for Web Services

In the context of the definition of Web services, a series of specific standards and proposal for standards exist, most of them propagated by the World Wide Web Consortium (W3C) or OASIS. To address the collection of these Web service-oriented specifications as a whole, they are usually addressed as "WS-*" specifications (the reason for this abbreviation might be the fact that the titles of many of these specifications contain the term "Web services" and have abbreviated identifications starting with "WS-").

A large number of WS-* specifications already exist, at different stages of their standardisation process, and the number of such specifications is still increasing.

---

58 ITU/UN, 2007
59 Rubin and Geer, 1998

Therefore, it is difficult to keep track of the dynamic development of these specifi-cations. However, an article in the InfoQ.com website provides a good overview of the state of standardisation and adoption by platform vendors as well as of the coherences and interdependencies of specifications in this field[60]. Unlike the exis-tence of several standardised business process definition languages that could basically replace each other, these different WS-* specifications serve different (though sometimes similar) purposes. Even though, overlapping functional areas also exist in these standards, proposals, or recommendations.

Since security issues are broadly accepted to be one of the crucial points in using Web services, in particular in cross-organisational application environments, there are also WS-* specifications specifically dedicated to the security aspects of Web services. Some of them will be discussed in more detail. The scope of existing security-related WS-* specifications covers the following aspects:

Specification of security requirements imposed to Web service invocation and mes-sage exchange between Web services or between Web services and their users.

Specification of protocols that may be used for security related tasks in the context of Web service-based application environments such as acquiring certified tokens for authentication and authorisation purposes or conveying information for access control purposes.

Specification of policies to determine the rules for granting or denying access to particular resources for particular principals (*i.e.*, users or other system resources acting on behalf of users)

3.1.1 Web Service Security (WS-Security)

Web Services Security usually addressed as WS-Security[61] is an OASIS standard adopted in 2004 and updated 2006 that provides the basis for secure message ex-change in Web service interoperation. The standard defines a security model for authentication and protection of the Simple Object Access Protocol (SOAP) mes-sage transfer and provides mechanisms, primarily within a special security header added to a SOAP message, to convey security-related content such as security to-kens or information as to which algorithms or procedures to be used for generation and verification of signatures or en-/decryption. Most of this standard describes mechanisms to be used for the following purposes:

- Specification of parts of a message and, in particular, of parts of the message header to be protected for integrity or confidentiality.
- Specification of method to be applied for encryption from a variety of alternate methods.

---

60 Bustamente, 2007
61 Nadalin *et al.*, 2006

WS-Security may be considered the base standard for security in this field since most of the other security-related WS-* specifications rely on the mechanisms provided by this standard to implement their security-oriented communication needs.

3.1.2   WS-SecurityPolicy

WS-SecurityPolicy[62], also an OASIS standard, offers means to indicate security requirements of Web services that have to be applied in the communication between the partners involved (*i.e.*, the invoker and the provider of a Web service). Such requirements may contain indications which parts of a message exchanged between the partners need protection to assure confidentiality or integrity and what type of encryption algorithms to be used for these purposes. In addition, means are provided to specify requirements for authentication and authorisation in message exchanges and what type of certifications will be accepted for these purposes. The mechanisms provided in this specification are predominantly bound to mechanisms provided in the communication layer of Figure 1, that is, the mechanisms provided by the communication protocol used. In many cases, this protocol will be SOAP[63] and its amendments, in particular WS-Security[64].

3.1.3   WS-Trust

WS-Trust[65] is another OASIS standard that specifies a model and procedures to acquire and exchange security credentials in such a way that communicating partners may establish and maintain a trust relationship between each other. The standard makes use of other WS-* specifications, in particular WS-Security and WS-Policy, and among others allows for secure exchange of security keys or policies.

3.1.4   Web Services Policy Framework (WS-Policy)

Web Services Policy Framework (WS-Policy)[66], is a W3C specification that may be used to construct policies relevant for a Web service. For this purpose the framework provides mechanisms for the aggregation of policies as combinations and alternatives of basic constraints and requirements of a Web service. The definition of such basic elements, however, is not in the scope of this specification but has to be imported from other WS-* specifications such as WS-SecurityPolicy[67] or WS-Security[68]. In addition to aggregation mechanisms, the framework specifies an algorithm for intersecting different policies in order to determine the common alter-

---

62 Nadalin *et al.*, 2007a
63 Box *et al.*, 2000
64 Nadalin *et al.*, 2006
65 Nadalin *et al.*, 2007b
66 Bajaj *et al.*, 2006
67 Nadalin *et al.*, 2007a
68 Nadalin *et al.*, 2006

natives contained in these policies. Although the mechanisms provided are not specific to security policies, the context of the specification and the examples used therein are bound to the field of Web service security.

3.1.5 Security Assertion Markup Language (SAML)

Security Assertion Markup Language (SAML[69] is again an OASIS standard for the specification and exchange of security assertions with respect to authentication, authorisation, or any relation between attributes and objects. Protocols for requesting assertions from an asserting party and for management of shared knowledge about identities between different providers acting as asserting parties are provided in this standard. One field of application of this standard is the establishment of so-called identity federations that play a central role in single sign-on over Web services from different providers.

3.1.6 eXtensible Access Control Markup Language (XACML)

The eXtensible Access Control Markup Language (XACML)[70] is also an OASIS standard that is intended to specify policies and procedures for access control and authorisation purposes. The standard provides a model for establishing access control decisions, an XML syntax for specifying access control policies as well as algorithms and functions that can be used in policy evaluation and constituting access control decisions.

The main components in the policy-based access control model are a Policy Enforcement Point (PEP) and a Policy Decision Point (PDP) that may be distributed over several nodes of a network. The PEP enforces access control based on policy decisions from the PDP. To this extent, the PEP sends decision requests to a PDP whenever access to a resource in the scope of the PEP is requested and receives responses containing the access decision from the PDP. While the structure and content of the decision requests and responses are specified in XACML, protocols for sending these requests and responses are not defined by this standard. Other standards such as SAML have to be employed for this purpose.

The decision request is accompanied by all required information concerning the requestor (subject), the resource access is requested for, the action requested to be performed on the resource, and the context (environment) in which the access request occurs. On receiving a decision request from a PEP, the PDP, in turn, evaluates rules contained in one or more policies (specified based on the schema provided in XACML for policy definition) that apply to the particular situation using the information contained in the decision request. The outcome of this evaluation may be "Permit", "Deny", "Indeterminate", or "NotApplicable" and is returned to the PEP in the response to a decision request. The PEP is responsible of enforcing

---

69 Cantor *et al.*, 2005
70 Moses, 2005

access control based on this decision by granting or denying access to the resource for the requestor.

Lorch *et al.*[71] report on early experiences with XACML in different application contexts. They discuss the use of XACML in its earlier version 1.0[72] in several projects and systems for authentication and authorization purposes. They conclude that XACML is suited for specifying complex policies and for being used in various distributed environments. Because it is an open standard offering means for extensibility, they argue that XACML fits well into legacy authentication and authorisation systems and may act as an intermediate for interoperability between different systems. They further conclude that the benefits gained by XACML's flexibility and expressiveness come at the cost of being complex and verbose (however, the latter applies similarly to many other XML-based standards, too). As a consequence, working directly with XACML policies "will be hard for average users"[73]. Even when tools will be available to cope with structural complexity and verbosity, the authors still suspect difficulties for users in understanding the meaning of policies expressed in XACML because of its inherent semantic complexity.

3.2   Role-Based Access Control for Web Services and Business Processes

While access control related aspects are predominant with Web services, they are, of course, also an issue with BPDLs. For Web services, role-based access control (RBAC)[74] is commonly used[75]. The main reason for this is that the maintenance effort increases tremendously with the number of principals (*i.e.*, users) and resources for access control systems relating decisions to grant or deny access to resources with individual principals as in conventional access control systems. Therefore, RBAC relating access decisions with particular roles instead of individual principals is better suited in situations involving a large number of principals as is the case in Web service environments[76]. In addition, since the users of Web services can be distributed over different organisations or are even unknown in advance, administration of access privileges for individual users would render difficult or even infeasible while associating possible invokers of a Web service with some few specific roles is much easier even with users from particular remote organisations and even with users that are unknown at the time the access rules are specified. However, even the supposed to be reduced effort for maintaining privileges of

---

71 Lorch *et al.*, 2003
72 Godik and Moses, 2003
73 *ibid.*, p. 34
74 Ferraiolo and Kuhn, 1992; Ferraiolo *et al.*, 1995
75 *e.g.*, Bacon *et al.*, 2002
76 Coetzee and Eloff, 2003

roles and associations between users and roles compared to the effort for maintaining privileges for all users individually has been criticised to increase considerably with complexity of IT infrastructure and if the number of users or privileges assigned to users tend to vary frequently. Hitachi[77] has stated that the effort for maintaining privileges of roles could even be higher than the possible economisation by avoiding maintenance of user privileges individually[78]. As an alternative, the authors propose on-demand assignment of privileges to users in combination with precautions against privilege accumulation. "Beyond roles" in the title of their paper addresses this economic aspect of privilege maintenance while "beyond RBAC" in the title of this book aims at overcoming functional limitations with respect to information flow control.

Organization-based access control (OrBAC)[79] is a framework based on similar principles as RBAC[80]. This framework has been developed for access and information control in the field of healthcare and social matters and aims to express security policies from different organisations in a common model. As a main amendment to RBAC, OrBAC introduces different types of contexts that allow for reducing a global set of rules contained in a security model to specific needs of different organisations.

Koshutanski and Massacci[81] address access control issues of business processes defined by BPEL scripts, in particular the problem of providing the evidence of possessing the required access privileges for accessing a particular resource at the right time to the right place during execution of a business process. In their approach, they propose to use mobile processes defined by BPEL scripts as part of messages sent in response to an access request. These mobile processes would be executed at the requesting side to interactively collect further credentials required for granting access to the particular resource. In this context, they also discuss the requirement that the mobile processes have to be subject to a release control policy in order to not disclose the access control policy unless the receiver of this information has already acquired the proper security level to be allowed to get this information. In order to deduce the missing credentials for an access request at a particular point of a business process and the required security level for disclosing the information which credentials currently are missing, the access control policy and the release control policy have to be available in a formulation that allows for machine-controlled reasoning. The authors argue that algebraic constructs would be best suited to serve as formal foundation for this purpose. However, requiring algebraic specifications for access control or release control policy makes the ap-

---

77 Hitachi, 2006
78 *ibid.*, p. 9
79 cf. OrBAC web site at www.orbac.org
80 Abou El Kalam *et al.*, 2003
81 Koshutanski and Massacci, 2003

proach difficult to be applied in practical applications where the skill to define or only understand such formal specifications of a policy cannot be considered to be commonly available with practitioners working in this field.

A similar aspect is addressed by Mendling *et al.*[82] in their investigation of access control requirements for BPEL script-defined business processes. By extracting RBAC models from BPEL scripts and converting BPEL language constructs in a format suitable for a particular RBAC software component, they provide an automated link of access control enforcement into business processes defined by the BPEL scripts.

Joshi *et al.*[83] give an overview of access control approaches and their suitability or usability for Web-based applications, in particular distributed workflow management systems (WFMSs). They argue that approaches such as the Mandatory Access Control (MAC)[84] and RBAC are suited for supporting enforcement of security policies in Web applications, particularly confidentiality and integrity of the information. In a MAC model, all subjects and objects are assigned predefined sensitivity levels to be used in the access control enforcement thereby including information flow control aspects into access control. For RBAC approaches to include information flow aspects, the concept of role hierarchies and constraints has to be employed. Joshi *et al.* state, "Enforcement of MAC policies is often a difficult task, and in particular for Web-based applications, they do not provide viable solutions because they lack adequate flexibility"[85]. They further state, "Achieving secure interoperation in a heterogeneous Web environment is a difficult task, because of the inherent dynamism and evolving security requirements of the underlying autonomous administrative domains"[86]. They come to the conclusion that extensions to RBAC models are required to adequately cope with security requirements in distributed Web application environments.

Peng and Chen[87] propose an extension to conventional RBAC models called WS-RBAC, in order to incorporate Web services and business processes on top of them. In their approach, Web services are subject to access control in lieu of common system resources in conventional approaches. Business processes and enterprises are elements in their WS-RBAC model making it suitable for application to CBPs.

---

82 Mendling *et al.,* 2004
83 Joshi *et al.,* 2001
84 Some authors treat MAC highly related to or even as synonym for Multilevel Security (MLS), *e.g.,* Miller *et al.,* 1997 or Knorr, 2001.
85 *ibid.,* p. 41
86 *ibid.,* p. 44
87 Peng and Chen, 2004

3.3   Relation of Programs and Programming Languages with Security Policies

Algebraic and language-based approaches, not specifically dedicated to Web services, address the relation of programs and programming languages with security policies. These papers address the issue of verifying compliance of programs with security policies and, therefore, their scope is comparable with the scope of consideration adopted in this book, albeit from a theoretical view.

Language-based techniques provide means for analysis or monitoring supported by properties or semantics of the particular programming or scripting language. Though the work concerned with these techniques relates to programming languages in general and is not particularly related to Web services or mobile code, the results of this work may also be extended thereto. At least, basic results on access control and information flow analysis, particularly on possible information leakage via certain semantics of programming languages, predominantly related to flow control semantics, also apply to the field of Web services and mobile code. A central role in the research on language-based security techniques is assigned to policies that restrict confidential data from interfering with (*i.e.,* affecting) public or externally observable data. This policy is referred to as noninterference[88].

Sabelfeld and Myers[89] give a comprehensive overview of language-based techniques for access control and, in particular, for information flow enforcement. They point out that access control on its own cannot guarantee confidentiality or noninterference of data. Sabelfeld and Myers argue that information flow analysis is required for enforcing confidentiality. This observation is in line with Joshi *et al.*[90] who argue that models based purely on access rules are not suitable for enforcing confidentiality and integrity of information after amendment, but access control model incorporating mechanisms for information flow control are able to do so. Sabelfeld and Myers also state that static information flow analysis is superior to dynamic information flow analysis since static analysis considers all possible execution paths of a program while dynamic analysis considers only one instance of program execution. They further argue that "the inability to express or enforce end-to-end security policies is a serious problem with our current computing infrastructure, and language-based techniques appear to be essential to any solution to this problem"[91]

One particular issue pointed out by Sabelfeld and Myers is the potential existence of so-called covert channels[92] and emphasise the difficulty to detect them during

---

88 Goguen and Meseguer, 1982
89 Sabelfeld and Myers, 2003
90 Joshi *et al.*, 2001
91 Sabelfeld and Myers, 2003, p. 13
92 Lampson, 1973

information flow analysis. Covert channels denote means for information transfer in a computing system that exploit mechanisms not primarily intended for information transfer. For instance, the number of cycles in a loop or the observation whether a particular exception occurs or not may be exploited to convey information in a manner not conforming to confidentiality policies. This may occur if looping or the condition for throwing a particular exception is based on confidential information thereby leaking this information via externally observable program behaviour.

An overview of algebraic approaches to access control has been given by Wijesekera and Jajodia[93]. While this work is dedicated mostly to theoretical aspects of security policies and their vulnerability by certain semantics of a programming language, enforcement of access control policies is stated as a requirement. However, mechanisms for doing so being, for instance, based on execution monitoring are not considered in this work.

Li and Zdancewic[94] consider confidentiality and integrity specified by information flow policies. They describe flow control analysis in a security policy context where so-called downgrading policies are established and enforced by the way of a type system using λ-calculus. The reason for considering downgrading policies as stated in their work is that noninterference being the only concept leads to overly strict limitation of allowed processing that would impede a lot of reasonable processing performed by a program. This theoretical approach to information flow analysis requires all programming logic being expressed in terms of λ-calculus in order to be analysed. In business processes invoking Web services for performing computational tasks or data manipulations, this approach seems to be impractical since, in general, it is unusual that formal specifications in terms of λ-calculus is available or can be made available for all of the programming logic contained in the Web services invoked during the course of a business process.

Another group of approaches to analysing confidentiality and integrity of programs written in different kinds of high-level languages investigate the information flow with respect to classified information. Within this group, type-based approaches and semantic-based approaches can be distinguished. In type-based approaches, for every security level an item of information may be assigned to, a certain type is defined and variables have to be of the same type as the information they contain. With these approaches, checking security properties such as noninterference can be performed by checking the type safety of a program[95].

---

93 Wijesekera and Jajodia, 2003
94 Li and Zdancewic, 2005
95 *e.g.*, Walker, 2000

Echahed and Prost[96] present an approach for proofing compliance of a program with information flow restrictions derived from a security policy. For their approach to be applicable, both the information flow restrictions and the program have to be available as algebraic formulations, the former using declarative programming, and the latter as rules of a term rewriting system. The information flow restrictions are formulated based on an ordered lattice of privacy levels where the order is defined from higher to lower privacy levels. This way, allowed or disallowed flows from higher to lower privacy level can be defined as rules in a term rewriting systems.

The approach described by Barbuti *et al.*[97] is another example of the semantic-based approaches. The authors address security of programs written in Java by checking the Java bytecode. In particular, they investigate a security property of Java programs called σ-security that is weaker than noninterference. The approach employs information flow analysis in abstract interpretation of the program. To this purpose, the semantics of each operation in Java bytecode are defined by inference rules. Given a partially ordered set of security levels and a particular threshold security level σ, they define a program being σ-secure, if only information assigned to security level σ and below are leaked by the program, while information of higher security levels be kept secret. In their information flow analysis, they also take into account the risk of covert channels called implicit flows in their approach as possible ways to disclose information. Abstract interpretation of a program considers the security levels of values stored in variables and in the stack instead of the concrete values. The authors prove that information flow analysis of all possible concrete traces of a program, that is the concrete transition system of the program, can be replaced by information flow analysis of abstract interpretation of the program.

Accorsi and Wonnemann[98] describe an approach to prevent unauthorised disclosure of information in business processes specified in BPEL or BPMN. Their approach is like our approach presented herein based on information flow analysis and, basically, is aiming at similar goals. To this end, processes defined by BPEL or BPMN are first transformed into coloured Petri nets (CPN). The CPNs then are analysed with respect to information leaks. The authors state that the dynamic analysis required for this purpose has exponential complexity with an order of $O(2^{3p})$ where p is the number of places in the Petri net analysed. Considering such increase of complexity with the number of places, the author argue that best practices in business processes would prescribe processes with at most 10 activities resulting in 11 places if transformed to Petri nets. They further argue that in practice not all places have to be considered potentially harmful, but only about five of

---

96 Echahed and Prost, 2005
97 Barbuti *et al.*, 2002
98 Accorsi and Wonnemann, 2010; Accorsi and Wonnemann, 2011

these places would have to be considered in the analysis. In their research, they used an implementation of this approach and show how this works in an example. However, in their second paper[99] the authors report that analysis performed with this implementation tends to cause false positive result. Given this and the complexity of handling Petri nets, which can by no means be considered commonplace, give rise to doubt whether this approach is actually suited to be applied in practice.

Strembeck and Mendling[100] describe an approach that allows for specifying business processes along with process-related access control policies. To this end, they define an algebraic metamodel for processes and process-related RBAC models. In this respect, their approach constitutes an extension of conventional RBAC. They further propose extensions to modelling languages such as UML to also include access control constraints related with the elements of the language, particular those representing activities. Their approach is intended to be applied in model-driven software development such that the process logic and the access policies can be mapped to software systems in a uniform manner. To assess the compliance of a process model to access control constraints involved, labelled transition systems similar to Petri nets are used to represent the behavioural semantics of the model. A reachability graph is derived from the models and analysed for potential deadlocks because their research has shown that absence of deadlocks is equivalent to compliance of process model to process-related RBAC model. Since this approach requires that business models and related access control constraints are specified in parallel, it might not be easy to be applied in the distributed definition and execution scenario of BPEL-based processes mainly considered here. Reason for this is that, at the specifying site, security policies of the executing site might not be available to deduce the process-related RBAC model and, even if they are, the site to execute the business process cannot be sure that the policies have been accounted for appropriately.

3.4 Verification of Consistency between Program Code and Security Policies

Another approach to cope with compliance of programs with security policy is based on the proposal, that programs are accompanied by information that proofs their compliance with particular security policies. Necula[101] proposed a scheme to extend a program by verifications that particular security policies are obeyed. This approach is known as Proof Carrying Code (PCC). The proof is performed by the supplier of the code and the executing side has the obligation to verify that the proof provided with the program holds. In order to provide the proof that certain

99   Accorsi and Wonnemann, 2011
100   Strembeck and Mendling, 2011
101   Necula, 1997

security requirements are met, the security requirements and a formal specification of the restrictions derived from them as well as of the program being executed are required. The proof that particular security requirements are obeyed may be supported by verifying compilation, that is, a compilation that verifies certain security-relevant properties of the code. While the proofs on the side of the producer of the mobile code are considered comparatively complicated, the verification of such proofs on the executing side is deemed to be comparatively simple. One important observation states that no trust relation is required between the producing and the executing side besides disclosing the security policy to the producing side. Proofs can only be conducted against known policies. Therefore, the policies have to be disclosed to the producer of the code. In order to embrace them in proofing particular security properties, the policies have to be formulated in a specific formalism in order to be used in formal reasoning.

A combination of the PCC approach with static analysis to overcome some shortcomings of pure PCC approaches has been proposed by Nordio *et al.*[102]. The main advantages of this approach are to provide proof of compliance if proofs based on type systems fail. The authors state that the size of proofs along their approach is linear to the size of the program considered. Since BPEL scripts usually are not compiled, this approach is of limited applicability to BPEL scripts since they are not going to be compiled before execution.

Walker[103] also considers certified code, where certification is based on strong type analysis as in Java. However, the approach goes beyond type checking by combining type checking with the approach of Schneider[104] that employs dynamic checking by code instrumentation. Such instrumentation adds specific code to enforce preconditions and postconditions of function invocations to be met.

Ribeiro *et al.*[105] describe a framework to specify security policies in a formal manner and methods to reason about the self-consistency of a security policy defined this way as well as about consistency between such a security policy and another set of rules or constraints. Such other sets of rules or constraints could, for instance, be derived from a workflow specification. In their approach, Ribeiro *et al.* define a Java-like notation for their policy definition language based on first-order predicate logic for specifying constraints with respect to allowed events. Ribeiro *et al.* show that a broad range of security policies including discretionary access control (DAC) and MAC policies may be expressed. For the purpose of verifying the consistency of a policy or of several policies they use a tool named Policy Consistency Verifier (PCV). This PCV operates as a term rewriting tool that is controlled by so-called Constraint Handling Rules (CHR) and a solver tool trying to verify different

---

102 Nordio *et al.*, 2004
103 Walker, 2000
104 Schneider, 2000
105 Ribeiro *et al.*, 2000

sets of constraint rules with respect to a set of consistency definitions. To verify the consistency of a workflow specified in a workflow definition language with a particular security policy, the policy first has to be specified in their specific security policy language. As a next step, this formal specification of the security policy and the formal specification of the workflow both have to be converted to sets of CHR rules. As a last step, the PCV tool is used to verify the consistence between these set of rules or detect their inconsistency. The authors state in their paper that compilers for the conversions of the formal specification of the security policy as well as the workflow into sets of CHR rules have been developed such that the verification process can be performed automatically using these compilers and their PCV tool. However, with respect to verifying consistency between workflows and security policy they concede that they "have not exhaustively tested with many different inconsistency types"[106]. Nevertheless, they state, "the results we have obtained so far and the flexibility of the underlying platform lead us to believe that PCV is able to find most types of inconsistencies within and between security policies and other specifications"[107].

3.5   Security Policy Enforcement via Code Instrumentation and Runtime Monitoring

The enforcement of security policies by means of code instrumentation and runtime monitoring is also a broadly used concept in several approaches in literature.

Schneider[108] discusses which kind of safety properties being part of security policies may be enforced by execution monitoring (EM) and finds that there are safety properties that may not be enforced by EM of such information flow properties. Like Sabelfeld and Myers[109], Schneider points out that security mechanisms based on static analysis and semantics of programming languages offer benefits over other approaches not using such mechanisms.

Venkatakrishnan *et al.*[110] propose a code-rewriting system for Java byte code to enable enforcement of security policies while executing mobile code. This approach aims at allowing for mobile Java code as much functionality as possible without violating security policies. In their system, security-relevant events are intercepted and forwarded to policy enforcement automata prior to execution. They argue that using extended finite state automata (EFSA) for the purpose of runtime monitoring of mobile code avoids the requirement for costly stack inspection techniques. As

---

106   *ibid.*, p. 11
107   *ibid.*, p. 12
108   Schneider, 2000
109   Sabelfeld and Myers, 2003
110   Venkatakrishnan *et al.*, 2002

being an approach particular to Java byte code, this approach is, in general, not suited to be applied to BPDL script-defined business processes.

A similar approach to the problem of executing untrusted code in general (*i.e.*, not specific to Java byte code or business process languages) was proposed by Sekar *et al.*[111]. After having derived information as to the behaviour of the code at the level of system calls from execution monitoring or static analysis at the developing site, this information is mapped to a model describing security-relevant behaviour and carried together with the code to the executing site where this information can both be checked against security policies and used during execution in order to monitor potential deviations from the stated behaviour. Applicability of this approach to business process running on a BPEL-enabled platform seems to be arguable because of lack of means to monitor system calls and relate them to specific activities of a particular business process. The requirement of extensive testing as explicitly stated in their paper and the need for observation at the level of system calls during execution, at least, will make the application of the approach in this context very complex.

Sirer and Wang[112] propose a system where policy enforcement code is derived from security policies by an enforcement machine and translated into platform-specific prologues and epilogues to Web service invocations. The specific enforcement code will be executed by the respective web server, thereby performing access control to Web services as required by security policies. This approach is limited to runtime checking of compliance of Web service invocations and security policies. If applied on its own, this approach shares the drawback of monitoring approaches that a possible violation of security policies may be detected too late to be prevented by intervention. However, if combined with other methods of security policy enforcement this kind of intervening programs may be supportive in order to prevent security policy violations.

In the approach of Vachharajani *et al.*[113], a specific runtime information flow engine is derived from binary program code prior to execution using special hardware that enables tracking of information flow. It provides dynamic information flow control during execution of program code thereby enabling access control policies or non-disclosure policies to be enforced. This approach, at least, requires binary code of the program being executed to be available for such 'instrumentation'. For Web services invoked by a business process, in particular in a distributed environment, access to binary program code cannot be assumed in general. Also when running business processes specified by BPDL scripts, the binary code being buried in the platform running these scripts may not be available for instrumen-

---

111 Sekar *et al.*, 2003
112 Sirer and Wang, 2002
113 Vachharajani *et al.*, 2004

tation. In general, the relation between sequences of binary code within the platform running a business process and particular parts of the business process is difficult to be determined. This is particularly true if such relations would be required prior to execution in order to enable instrumentation of the appropriate parts of the binary code.

3.6   Classification of Approaches to Security Policy Enforcement

The approaches discussed in this chapter can be categorised by the level at which they are applied. The first category comprises the approaches that act directly upon the scripts or programs executed and enforcement of security policies usually requires no conversion of the rules contained in these policies in order to become operable for the measures applied for this purpose. This situation is depicted in Figure 5. Some approaches add further information to the program or script providing directions as to how compliance to applicable security policies can be assured at runtime. Other approaches adopt code instrumentation to support security policy enforcement, but still act at the level of the program or script under consideration. Approaches in this category predominantly are applied at runtime.

Figure 5: Compliance Assessment at Script/Program Level

Approaches that exercise security policy enforcement at runtime suffer the risk that violation of restrictions implied by security policies might be detected too late for an intervention that could effectively prevent harm. The approaches discussed in Sections 3.2 and 3.5 all fall into this category as well as some approaches discussed in Section 3.4.

A second category includes approaches that do not act at the program or script level, but are applied at an abstract level. As shown in Figure 6, these methods are applied on formal representations of the security policies as well as of the program logic of the program or script under consideration that, obviously, have to be available for that purpose. The approaches introduced in Section 3.3 and some of the approaches in Section 3.4 are representatives of this type of policy enforcement. In order to get formal representations of program logic and security policies, transformations of the program or script as well as of the security policies need to be performed To deduce a formal description from a program or script is complicated and not easy to be achieved in practice, in particular with real world programs or scripts that tend to be considerably larger than those typically used as examples or for proof of concept in research.

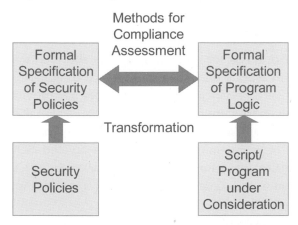

Figure 6: Compliance Assessment at Abstract Level

Approaches providing methods to assure that a formal representation of a program based on a model complies with security policies to be observed similarly available as formal representation also fall into this category. Here, compliance assessment is performed at an abstract level before conversion into an executable representation takes place. Such formal representations of programs typically are available in model driven development. The complicated transformation of a program into a formal representation as mentioned above can be avoided in this situation. However, for the compliance with security policies to remain valid after having been assessed at a formal level, conversion to executable programs or scripts have to be performed in such a manner that no deviation from the behaviour with respect to abidance of security policies can be introduced into the executable version. This requires that conversion is performed in exactly defined way. Usually, such conversion could also be and, in fact, often will be performed automatically, for instance, during model driven development. In many cases, conversion of a design model into executable pieces of code is only suited for automatic performance up to a certain degree and, therefore, needs to be completed manually. This manually executed part of conversion bears the risk to introduce deviation from the formally described behaviour of the program that could even cause violation of security policies and, thereby, could invalidate the assessed compliance from the abstract level..

These methods predominantly are based on algebraic representations of the program or script as well as of the security policies. Though some of these methods are described to have been supported by tools in the respective research projects, such approaches using algebraic representations, in general, are not easy to apply and, even if supported by tools, the results delivered by those tools are not easily verifiable by the users. In addition, the tools reported to having been used in the research projects might not be available to users who want to apply these approaches in practice.

3.7 Summary

As the discussion of the WS-* specifications for security purposes above shows, most of these specifications deal with aspects related to Web service communication and access control. Since BPEL as a specification language does not provide elements that address access control and secure communication (cf., Section 4.2), these aspects of business process execution are expected to be provided by the platform running these processes[114]. Therefore, if mapped onto the layered SOC architecture in Figure 1, mechanisms required for these tasks reside in the layers below the business process layer, that is, the content layer and the communication layer.

With the exception of WS-Policy and XACML, which may be used for specifying any kind of security policy, these standards do not address aspects that are relevant to the scope of our considerations, namely assessment of BPEL scripts with respect to compliance with security policies.

Concerning WS-Policy and XACML, since they address policy definition, they could be employed as standardised means to specify security policies when a BPEL script is checked for compliance with them. However, it turned out that they were not considered to be advantageously employed in the context of the novel method presented in this book. The reasons for this will be discussed in more detail in Chapter 4.

Also other approaches to the specification of security requirements of Web services as discussed in Section 3.2 address aspects residing in layers 1 and 2 of Figure 1 or they are dedicated to the second security issue in the list of Section 2.3. Therefore, they are not applicable to the security issue stated in the first item of the list in Section 2.3 being the main scope of consideration adopted for this book.

The approaches in Sections 3.3 and 3.4 do not specifically address security aspects of remotely defined BPEL scripts. Since all these approaches are based on algebraic formulations on programming language semantics and security policies, they are not particularly suited to be applied by practitioners in the field of Web service definition and business process specification. The specific skill required to define and interpret such formal specification may not generally be anticipated to be available for people occupied with specifying Web services and business processes.

Despite the observation that most of the results from other research mentioned in this section do not particularly address distributed definition and deployment of BPEL scripts in the sense laid out in Chapter 2, some of their approaches may also

---

114 cf., *e.g.*, Mendling *et al.*, 2004

be applicable to this topic, at least to a certain extent. Particularly, results concerned with access control, in general, and access control to Web services, in particular, may be applicable to the second security aspect arising in this context as listed in Section 2.3. The considerations in this book, however, are aimed to address the first security aspect in this list. It will turn out that approaches beyond RBAC using methods and procedures that are easy to apply in practice will be required to satisfactorily cope with this security aspect.

Furthermore, the observation by several authors that access control on its own is insufficient for enforcing confidentiality and integrity of information as well as the potential risk of covert channels as discussed above in Section 3.3 was adopted in the development of the methods presented in the following chapters.

Except of the approach of Accorsi and Wonnemann[115], which besides its exponential complexity lead to false positive results in experimental implementation by the authors and, therefore, gives rise to doubt its appropriateness in practice, none of the results discussed in this chapter deals specifically with the first security aspect indicated in Section 2.3 (which is the main concern of the novel methods presented in the following chapters). Some of the work on language-based techniques for information flow control and on instrumentation and monitoring, nevertheless, are applicable to this aspect, at least in principle. However, as already discussed above, the algebraic and language-based approaches mentioned may only be of limited use in the business process context because of the program size of the platform running business processes. The fact that program logic of Web services involved is only known up to a certain degree and, in general, is far away from being specified in an algebraic formalism that would be required for most of these algebraic approaches further stands in the way of applying such approaches for the purposes considered here.

Because of the fast pace of development and updating or reworking cycles that seems to be typical for Web services and business processes, it may be disputed whether such formal algebraic specifications will be produced in the future for applications in this field. In addition, at least for the time being, skills required for providing such algebra-based formulation seem not to be typically available when developing Web services and business processes.

The approaches presented in the following chapters, therefore, aimed to provide methods for analysing and assessing security-relevant semantics of BPEL scripts that may be applied without requiring profound skills in special formalisms such as algebraic formulation of programming logic. By contrast, the methods developed were to be based on technology and methods well-known to developers of Web services and business processes in order to be comparatively easy to be applied and, therefore, can be expected to be adopted by practitioners in this field.

---

115 Accorsi and Wonnemann, 2010; Accorsi and Wonnemann, 2011

The next chapters present the approaches taken in order to reach this aim. To start with, BPEL is analysed with respect to its intrinsic potential to specify behaviour of business processes that could violate restrictions imposed by security policies.

4 Analysis of Security-Relevant Semantics of BPEL

In this section, the results of an analysis of BPEL as a specification language will be presented. The purpose of this analysis was to identify the intrinsic potential of BPEL to specify business process behaviour that is able to violate restrictions imposed by security policies. These results form the basis for the methods and procedures for security policy assessment introduced in the next chapter. Readers familiar with syntax and semantics of BPEL as a specification language may skip the overview in Section 4.2.

Here and in the following chapters, the term "security relevance" when used with respect to particular elements of a programming or scripting language (*e.g.*, BPEL) or to combinations of such elements denotes the potential of these elements or combinations thereof to specify behaviour of a program (or a business process in the case of BPEL) that could violate a security policy-implied restriction. Once the security-relevant semantics of BPEL have been identified, the assessment of compliance between a BPEL-defined business process and a particular security policy will become more operable since checking the BPEL script for compliance can be restricted to looking for security-relevant semantics contained therein.

4.1 Scope of Analysis

For the sake of general applicability, the aim is to analyse security relevance of semantics expressible via BPEL as a specification language as broadly as possible, without referring to specific types of application to which a particular BPEL script-defined business process may be related. For this purpose, the smallest possible pieces of BPEL scripts had to be identified for which assertions with respect to security relevance could sensibly be made. This cannot be the language constructs of BPEL on their own because, similar to many other programming languages or scripting languages, most or even all of the individual language constructs do not present any security relevance or the security relevance cannot be determined at this "atomic" level.

As can be easily seen, for instance, the security relevance of an assignment operator or command (as present in nearly all programming or scripting languages) cannot be determined if considered in isolation since an assignment operation simply copies values from one location to another usually within registers or main memory of a computer. In order to decide the security relevance of such an operation, further information on the values and the locations involved in this operation is required such as what kind of values are to be copied (*e.g.*, values representing security-classified information) and what operation are to be performed to the target location during the further processing of the program (*e.g.*, stored on an externally accessible storage or displayed to a user on a terminal screen). If considered together with the restrictions that could be imposed to the values and locations involved, the security relevance of an assignment operation becomes easier to be investigated, but still it is not generally decidable for all types of restrictions whether an operation is secure or not.

The whole of a specific program and even the environment in which the program will be executed may have to be considered to decide this. For instance, if the values copied represent information that is restricted by the security policy to not be leaked to users of the program unless they possess a special authorisation to access this information and the target location would be known to get displayed on a user terminal in the further processing of the program, also knowledge about the environment in which the program will be executed would be required to decide whether the assignment operation violates the security policy or not. If the environment assures that only appropriately authorised persons have access to the room where the particular terminal is installed then the operation may be considered secure. If, however, also people without such authorisation may watch the screen where this information is going to be displayed, that is the environment does not provide measures to avoid this, then the assignment operation would have to be considered insecure.

Admittedly, approaches to security analysis of a programming language usually do not claim to be so far-reaching as to also include considerations concerning the prospective environmental conditions of program execution, but are based on implicit or explicit expectations that these conditions will be appropriate to support security requirements, for example, to prevent inadvertently leakage of information to observers not adequately authorised. Also in this analysis, considerations with respect to environmental conditions as mentioned above will be out of scope. As usual in this type of analyses it is anticipated that appropriately secure environmental conditions are provided by the organisation running the platform on which a business process is to be executed. Since herein a specification language at business process level is subject to the analysis, which is unable to directly present any information to users (this could, at most, be achieved indirectly via messages sent to a Web service or to an invoker of a business process, which usually is also a program), this approach is particularly justified.

4.1.1   Search for Security-Relevant Building Blocks of BPEL Semantics

From the above considerations, combinations of the language constructs with typical restrictions implied by security policies were deemed to be suitable as the smallest parts of BPEL scripts for which sensible statements with respect to their security relevance could be established. Before examining the semantics of these combinations, restrictions derived from security policies for BPEL-defined business processes have been investigated. From this investigation, categories or classes of such policy-derived restrictions have been determined at the abstraction level at which a business process is specified and executed on an appropriate platform.

It turned out that the combination of language constructs of BPEL with classes of restrictions derived from security policies were suitable to identify the security-relevant features of BPEL. The analysis shows that only a subset of the language constructs entails the risk to violate certain classes of restrictions while the rest do not possess any security relevance.

The knowledge of the security-relevant language features in terms of combinations of restriction classes and BPEL constructs provides a clear conception what to look for when analysing a BPEL script for compliance with security policies. In this way, assessment of compliance with security policy is considerably facilitated since a thorough analysis of each and every particular aspect of the semantics of a BPEL script under consideration and comparison with security policy is no longer required. Instead, a direct scan of a BPEL script looking only for the features identified to be capable of violating the security policy will be sufficient for this purpose. Classifying the restrictions derived from the rules in a particular security policy and relating them with their relevance for BPEL scripts will further make the assessment easier to handle since only those rules in such a policy remain to be considered that are applicable at the level of business process execution.

4.1.2   Trade-Off Between Policy Strictness and Functional Richness

To allow as much functionality as possible in a business process within the limitations imposed by security policies, it is postulated that the restrictions derived from such policies shall be as weak as possible, but at the same time as strict as required to avoid any violation of security policies. This requires a fine-grained concept of specifying access restrictions and information flow restrictions. If, for instance, all internal Web services of the gearbox manufacturer in the example of Figure 4 would either be allowed or forbidden to be invoked by a business process brought into domain B by the car manufacturer, then only such process logic could be specified by a cross-domain deployed BPEL script that could also be performed when running the BPEL script within domain A of the car manufacturer. The only additional requirement for this to happen would be that access would be admitted across the security domain border between the car manufacturer and the gearbox manufacturer for those Web services that were allowed to be accessed in a BPEL script from the car manufacturer when running in domain B.

Though the difficulties to allow such cross-domain access to particular Web services from within domain A (*e.g.*, difficulties to re-define rules for mechanisms controlling remote access to Web services, typically firewall rules, in such a way that in addition to access privileges to the particular Web services existing before, access would only be allowed for invocations from domain A) could already justify the cross-organisational deployment of a BPEL script, the more interesting cases involve fine-grained access or information flow restrictions. Such restrictions may allow access to a Web service only if passing values returned by former invocations of other Web services or allow information returned by a Web service only to be used in a specific way.

These kind of restrictions could not be controlled if the business process were running outside domain B unless the existing Web services (or at least some of them) would be changed considerably. Without modifications to the Web services in domain B to provide additional mechanisms for authentication and integrity-protection of values passed to a Web service, the source of input values to a Web service invoked from domain A could not be determined by a control mechanism residing in domain B. Similarly, without additional mechanisms for providing confidentiality, values returned across the domain border could not be controlled by domain B as to where they are going to be used in domain A. Allowing cross-organisational deployment of the script defining the business process and checking the script for compliance with the restrictions implied by such fine-grained rules for access control and information flow control would avoid modification to existing Web services and the computational overhead to provide the security mechanisms mentioned above.

4.1.3   Need for Information Flow Analysis in Policy Compliance Assessment

Since the strategy of compliance assessment aims at avoidance of any infringement of security policies, following Dobson[116] access control and information flow control are the mechanisms to be applied. While access control with respect to the Web services invoked during the execution of the business process and the flow of information from and to these Web services and from and to its environment are to be considered, access control to the Web service offered by the business process under consideration to its environment (being the concern of a complementary security issue as indicated in Section 2.3) was not in the scope of these considerations. Hence, the analysis was refined to examining whether information or resources accessed and the flow of information within a business process are consistent with the limitations of the security policy.

The investigation of restrictions to business processes (in particular those defined remotely from the location of intended execution) imposed by security policy came up with following aspects addressed by them:

- Access control as a whole or to particular parameters of a Web service
- Information flow control as a whole or to particular parameters of a Web service

While the decision whether access to a resource is allowed within the limitations of a policy is comparatively easy to define, distinguishing allowed and disallowed

---

116 Dobson. 1994, p. 11

information flow needs further consideration. As discussed in Chapter 3, many approaches addressing information flow control policies use the concept of classified information sources and sinks in order to investigate and even prove noninterference (*i.e.*, the property of a program that no information flow exists from higher to lower security levels)[117] or that such information flow occurs only in a controlled fashion[118]. As stated by Joshi *et al.*[119] , MAC and RBAC (the latter with role hierarchies and constraints) also make use of classified information and thereby allow for information flow control between different levels.

4.1.4 Approach to Dispensability of Security Classification System

To avoid unnecessarily complicating matters, the approach taken here does not explicitly make use of a more or less elaborate classification system of information and resources, but instead simply differentiates between allowed and disallowed information flows in terms of Web service invocations and message exchange with invokers of a business process. To further simplify the definition of allowed and disallowed information flow, it is assumed that

- information flow restrictions in the forward direction (see below for an explanation) are not required within the domain executing the business process (referred to as the executing domain),
- all Web services (both inside and outside the executing domain) a business process is allowed to invoke are explicitly identified,
- restrictions to information flow in the forward direction relate to all external sinks (*i.e.*, information flow crossing domain boundaries is generally affected by such restrictions, possibly with some indicated exceptions) while internal sinks are excepted from these kind of restrictions for information coming from the same domain, and
- restrictions to information flow in the backward direction relate to particular sources information has to originate from or restricts information to comply with a particular range of allowed values.

Note: It may be argued that the second aspect of the last item should rather be considered an access restriction than an information flow restriction. For the purpose of the discussion herein, and in the following chapters, it does not matter whether a restriction to a particular set of allowed values is treated as belonging to access control or to information flow control.

Thereby, use of classified information is made only implicitly, avoiding the need of defining a classification system (or making use of an existing one) and assigning classes or levels from this system to all resources and users or roles involved in a

---

117 *e.g.*, Sabelfeld and Myers, 2003
118 Chong and Myers, 2004; Li and Zdancewic, 2005
119 Joshi *et al.*, 2001

business process. As a consequence of the assumptions on information flow rules stated above, the implied classification system basically consists of the following security levels:

- information sinks and resources inside the executing domain;
- information sinks and resources outside the executing domain.

However, whenever requirements for a refined classification system occur, refinement takes place implicitly by stating information flow restrictions or indicating relaxations of general restrictions implied by those assumptions. Since no explicit use of classified information is made when stating information flow rules, there is no need for adapting a classification system prior to making use of its refined version. Therefore, such rules can be formulated as required without caring about predefined security levels and formal aspects of level-crossing information flows.

Besides simplifying the definition of information flow restrictions, this approach also helps to facilitate assessment of compliance with these rules. Since nearly all sinks and sources of information in BPEL-defined business processes are bound to Web services invoked and messages exchanged with invokers of the business process (*i.e.*, invocation of this process' Web service from its environment). Rules formulated in terms of restrictions to Web service invocations, and the information flow related thereto, cover most of the information flow restrictions that apply at all. In addition to explicit information flow to and from Web services and the environment of the business process, the possibility for covert channels is to be taken into account during information flow analysis of a BPEL script since also implicit information flow violating any restriction has to be avoided.

Information flow analysis in the forward direction is understood to consider the flow of information from the point in time during execution that a particular piece of information is brought into a business process (*e.g.*, output of a Web service invocation returned to the business process) to destinations this particular piece of information could flow to in the further processing of the process. By contrast, information flow analysis in the backward direction is understood to consider the flow of information from any sources introducing pieces of information into a process in the past before the point in time that such pieces of information are passed to a particular sink (*e.g.*, input to a Web service invoked by the business process). Put simply, backward information flow analysis is concerned with the past and forward information flow analysis is concerned with the future of information involved at a particular point during business process execution.

4.1.5   Risks of Policy Violations of Remotely Defined Business Processes

As motivated by the discussion in Section 3.1 relating to security aspects of Web services that can be expressed in the framework provided by WS-* specification, such security requirements are to a large extent dealt with at layers below the business process layer in Figure 1 (namely at the communication layer and the content layer). In particular, access control requirements to Web services as a whole and to parts of the resources and information made available by them may be treated in these layers. However, when remotely defined BPEL scripts are running within the security domain they may inherit access privileges from the local environment. As a consequence, access attempts from within the business process may pass the control mechanisms in the lower layers and be granted in a way not intended for such remotely defined business processes. Therefore, in addition to security policy rules typically applicable to the business process layer, the scope of the analysis of such remotely defined BPEL scripts for potential conflicts with local security policies has to be broadened to accommodate this special situation. In particular, it has to pay attention to policy violations that will made possible by the fact that these scripts are executed within the local security domain, but would have been prevented by other (usually access control) mechanisms in layers below the business process layer if executed outside (*e.g.*, in the domain where they were defined). Risks of policy violations by those cross-domain deployed BPEL scripts fall into one of the following categories:

- making information or use of resources available outside the executing domain beyond the limitations imposed by the policy (*e.g.*, reading information with restrictions relating to forward information flow from a database and sending it to an external partner);
- bringing information from outside into an internal data storage that is not allowed to be written to from external sources; and
- using functionality or resources that are not allowed to be used (*e.g.*, altering data in a data base or exercising a system control function).

In the following sections of this chapter, after an overview of BPEL as a specification language, security policy-induced restrictions to Web service invocation are categorised and combined with BPEL constructs. The aim herein is the identification of security-relevant building blocks of business process behaviour specified by such combinations.

4.2 Overview of BPEL Semantics

The standardised business process definition language BPEL has been brought into an OASIS standardisation process based on a proposition that originated from merging two vendor-specific BPDLs, namely Microsoft's XLANG[120] and IBM's WSFL[121]. The approaches to specify business process logic were different in these two BPDLs and as a compromise in the standardisation process, BPEL still contains the different approaches to express business logic inherited from these two vendor-specific predecessors. This is the reason why BPEL (in the version adopted as an

---

120 Thatte, 2001
121 Leymann, 2001

OASIS standard[122]) still comprises two essentially different ways of expressing process flow logic. These are a graph-structured modelling style inherited from WFSL and a block-structured modelling style inherited from XLANG.

During the course of the research resulting in the approaches presented here, the definition of BPEL has undergone some modifications. While the discussion in this chapter is based on the version 2.0 of BPEL, which finally has been accepted as OASIS standard[123], the prototype is based on previous versions of BPEL specifications. The reasons for this and why this is not deemed to void the proof of concept that has been aimed to be achieved will be discussed in Chapter 7.

Basically, BPEL only provides means for specifying Web service invocation and the exchange of messages with the environment of the business process being specified as well as means for specifying the flow of control and information between these invocations and message exchanges. In addition, BPEL comprises means to specify what should happen when exceptions are raised or errors occur.

While a detailed description of BPEL can be found in its specification[124], a comprehensive analysis of its semantics was conducted by Wohed *et al.*[125] based on a previous version of the BPEL specification. An overview of the language and a comprehensive example is given by Leymann and Roller[126]. The nature of BPEL accommodates the analysis of security-relevant semantics by offering only little or no means for defining data processing or computational tasks as part of the language itself. For these purposes, BPEL scripts have to invoke Web services, or must import constructs from other XML standards such as XQuery[127], XSLT[128], or XPath[129]. In addition, security aspects such as authentication, provision of secure communication channels, and non-repudiation do not have to be considered in this context, since the language does not provide any means related to these security aspects. These aspects usually are catered for by the platform running BPEL scripts. Thus, the analysis can be concentrated on the business or workflow logic that may be expressed in BPEL in order to identify security-relevant semantics.

In BPEL, two types of processes may be modelled: executable and abstract processes. Abstract processes are used to specify a business protocol in order to define the potential sequence of messages exchanged between business partners. Since such protocols should allow the internals of business processes actually performed by the partners to be hidden, abstract processes may comprise some kind of vague-

122 Alves *et al.*, 2007
123 OASIS, 2007
124 Alves *et al.*, 2007
125 Wohed *et al.*, 2002
126 Leymann and Roller, 2004
127 Boag *et al.*, 2007
128 Kay, 2007
129 Berglund *et al.*, 2006

ness with respect to process logic performed internally by the business partners. Since abstract processes are not executable by their definition, they are not in the scope of this analysis where BPEL scripts intended for actual execution on a remote platform are considered.

Therefore, only executable processes are subject to this analysis. BPEL scripts intended for this purpose specify workflow logic in terms of activities. The prevalent semantics expressed in BPEL is the exchange of messages with one or several external partners that can be thought of as invoking Web services provided by partners or being invoked as a Web service by partners. In a declaration part, BPEL scripts define the potential links to external partners by references to WSDL definitions of the Web services involved. Thus, analysing these declarations in a first step yields the set of Web services that may be invoked or are offered by a business process under consideration.

4.2.1 General Structure of BPEL Scripts

In BPEL, like in high level programming languages, there exists a predefined structure of several groups of declarations serving different purposes. Each BPEL script represents an instance of an XML element `<process>` that may contain several parts for defining elements not directly related to normal process flow (except event handlers, cf. explanation below) and one element specifying the process logic of the business process called an activity. This single activity at the top level of a process definition is usually a structured one, which means an activity containing other activities. The parts not directly related to normal process flow are all optional (though at least some of them are required to compose a BPEL script defining a proper process). These parts contain declarations of the interfaces to the environment of the business process (called partner links in BPEL), the variables to be used, and so-called event handlers and fault handlers. In addition, some of these parts may define links to other specifications via XML namespace definitions and by explicit import via an `<import>` element or even extensions of process logic not expressible with BPEL-defined activities. In particular, declarations of partner links refer to WSDL definitions of Web services to be invoked by a business process or defining the Web service provided by the business process specified in a BPEL script. Also the declaration of variables may refer to WSDL definitions but also may be related to definitions of arbitrary XML schemas. The latter is new in BPEL 2.0 since in former versions of BPEL variables were only allowed to be declared in terms of types imported from WSDL definitions.

While the other declaration parts do not contain any process logic and, therefore, only indirectly influence security-relevant semantics of BPEL, event handlers and fault handlers directly contribute to the process logic. Fault handlers are intended to define process logic to be performed in response to exceptions and errors that may occur during the execution of the normal process. Besides indicating the condition for being selected and executed (*i.e.,* specifying the fault to which a handler reacts), fault handlers specify process logic using activities as in the part specifying the normal process flow. In addition, there are some activities especially reserved to only be used within fault handlers. Since the occurrence of a fault is not considered normal in a process definition, fault handlers specify exceptional process behaviour that might never be executed if no exception or error caught by any of these handlers occurs. However, since occurrence of such faults cannot be ruled out during the analysis and since these faults may occur unpredictably at any time during process execution, all process logic specified in such fault handlers may be deemed to represent potential parallel flows to the normal flow of the process and may be treated as such when analysing a BPEL script for compliance with security policies.

Event handlers also specified in the declaration part of a `<process>` element specify how a process should react when particular events occur such as incoming messages or timeout events. On one hand side like fault handlers, event handlers specify the event or the timeout condition that trigger their process logic to be executed. On the other hand side, unlike fault handlers these declarations specify not exceptional, but normal behaviour of a process and, therefore, have to be considered an integral part of the normal flow of process logic. The semantics of such event handlers is very similar to those of the `pick` activity, which will be discussed below. As with fault handlers, the trigger events specified in such a handler may occur at any time during process execution and, thus, the process logic of these handlers may be thought of as potential parallel flows to the process logic specified in the main process stream specified in the BPEL script.

4.2.2   Primitive and Structured Activities in Normal Process Flow

The activities expressing the semantics of a process either in the main stream or in the exceptional or event-triggered streams of a business process may be either primitive or structured. BPEL provides the following primitive activities to be used in the normal flow of process logic (*i.e.*, the process flow collectively specified in the activity of the main stream and the event handlers in contrast to exceptional process flow specified in fault handlers):

- `invoke`   invocation of a Web service
- `receive`   waiting for a message to arrive
- `reply`   sending a reply to a message received
- `assign`   assignment of values between two different locations
- `wait`   waiting for a specified amount of time
- `throw`   indication of exceptions such as failures during execution
- `exit`   termination of a process instance. (Note: Was `terminate` in previous versions of BPEL)
- `validate`   validation of the content of variables against their type definition in WSDL documents or XML schemas
- `empty`   no operation

The structured activities provided by BPEL are:

- `sequence`   definition of a fixed execution order
- `flow`   parallel execution of activities
- `if`   branching between several alternate activities depending on conditions. (Note: Replaces the `switch` activity of previous versions of BPEL)
- `while`   iterative execution, *i.e.*, looping as long as loop condition holds
- `repeatUntil`   iterative execution, *i.e.*, looping provided loop condition holds. (Note: Added during standardisation process of version 2.0)
- `forEach`   iterative execution, *i.e.*, multiple execution for a specified number of iterations either consecutively or in parallel. (Note: Added during standardisation process of version 2.0)
- `pick`   waiting simultaneously for several events to occur and proceeding depending on the event that actually occurs; typically, one event waited for is a timeout event

4.2.3   Additional Flow Control and Structuring Elements

Additional control of parallel and sequential flows within a `flow` activity may be expressed by so-called links (not to be confused with partner links) that are used to specify dependencies and sequencing of parallel flows. The language constructs applicable for this purpose are:

- `links`   definition of links to be used within a flow activity (not to be confused with partner links defining external interfaces)
- `source`   used to specify an activity to be a predecessor of another one
- `target`   used to specify an activity to be a successor of another one

Listing 1: Graph-Structured Modelling

```
<flow>
 <links>
  <link name="reverse"/>
 </links>
 <activity2>
  <target linkName="reverse"/>
 </activity2>
 <activity1>
  <source linkName="reverse"/>
 </activity1>
</flow>
```

Listing 2: Block-Structured Modelling

```
<sequence>
 activity1
 activity2
</sequence>
```

In the examples in Listings 1 and 2, the graph-structured and block-structured modelling provided by BPEL are compared. It should be noted that both examples, though one uses a `flow` activity and the other uses a `sequence` activity, result in identical process semantics. This is caused by the `link` element used in Listing 1. Although the example activities `activity1` and `activity2` which actually serve as placeholders for any BPEL activity occur lexically in reverse order within the `flow` activity, they will be executed in the same order as in the `sequence` activity of Listing 1 due to the `link` named `reverse`. By defining the activity occurring first within the flow as the target of this link while the activity occurring second is defined as the source of the same link, the actual execution order of these two activities will be reversed. Note that reversion of execution order is not effectuated by the name of this link, but only by the way this link is used as a target and source, respectively, in both activities.

In addition to structured activities, there is another language construct, named `scope`, similar to structured activities since it also serves structuring purposes but is not considered a structured activity (however, terminology in BPEL standard[130] is not consistent with respect to this). This construct is used to define nested structures of scopes for the declaration of particular constructs. Actually, a scope provides virtually the same structure for the declaration of partner links, variables, fault handlers, event handlers, and a single activity as the `<process>` element which may be considered the top-level scope of the hierarchy of nested scopes. In addition, two other types of declarations are particular to scopes – namely termination handlers and compensation handlers[131]. Each scope definition may contain at most one of each of these declarations. The purpose of these declarations is to specify process logic in the case of (normal) termination of the activity defined in a `scope` or in the case the activity of a `scope` needs kind of roll back, called compensation in BPEL. Rolling back the effects of a (usually structured) activity of a `scope` could be required in response to an error occurring during the execution of this `scope`. Typically, activities to be reversed by a compensation handler are those that have been performed within the particular scope to which the compensation handler refers.

4.2.4   Special Activities for Fault Handling

There are some further primitive activities, `compensate` and `compensateScope`, collectively referred to as compensation activities used to initiate rollback actions in transaction-based application contexts, and `rethrow` for passing faults to the enclosing nesting level. They are only allowed to be used within fault handlers. Since compensation activities initiate the execution of one or several compensation handlers they logically link activities defined in such handlers to fault handlers containing these compensation activities. While `compensateScope` is intended to initiate the compensation for a particular scope, `compensate` initiates compensation for the scope related to fault handler issuing this activity as well as for all nested scopes within this containing scope. The `rethrow` activity passes the infor-

---

130   Alves *et al.*, 2007

131   The concept of termination handlers is new in version 2.0. For compensation handlers, there used to be the possibility to define them at process level in former BPEL versions, but this has been removed in the final version of BPEL 2.0

mation that a particular exception occurred possibly accompanied by some fault variable containing further information to its containing scope level or to the process level. Therefore, a `rethrow` activity needs attention in information flow analysis with respect to the fault variable and the exception passed to the next higher nesting level.

4.2.5 Concept of Multiple Instantiation in BPEL

In addition to the activities representing the main part of the semantics of BPEL, there is a concept of multiple instantiation in BPEL that enable several instances of the same business process being defined by one script and being created by messages arrival from external partners. As long as the different instances do not share common variables that is usually not the case though the standard does not compel that each instance uses a separate copy of its variables, these instances may be considered separate copies of the same BPEL script running in parallel. Therefore, multiple instantiation does not add any particular security relevance and, therefore, no particular consideration of multiple instantiation is required during this analysis. Instead, the results applicable for a BPEL script not using multiple instantiation can be applied to each copy independently whether it runs as separate processes or as instances of a single process. If several instances should communicate with each other, this is performed via mutual message exchange as with external Web services invoked by a business process and, thus, does not represent any special case not considered otherwise in this analysis. In essence, multiple instantiation will not be investigated separately and only the requirement is stated that multiply instantiated processes shall not share identical variables because doing so could impose covert channels.

4.2.6 Extensibility of BPEL and Problems for Compliance Assessment Involved

BPEL provides extensibility in several ways. First, BPEL allows for namespace-qualified attributes in any BPEL element and also elements from arbitrary namespaces to appear within elements defined in BPEL. Further, BPEL 2.0[132] provides three elements for explicitly defining extensions within a BPEL script. These elements are `extensions`, `extensionActivity`, and `extensionAssignOperation` the last one occurring as part of an `assign` activity. The standard clearly defines the conditions when a BPEL implementation may ignore such extensions, but still execute the rest of the script containing these extensions and when it is required to reject a BPEL script for execution that contains particular extensions not supported by the implementation.

Obviously, for the purpose of assessing the compliance of a BPEL-defined business process with local security policies, the presence of any extension in a BPEL script

---

132 Alves *et al.*, 2007

is detrimental since it introduces new semantics that could not be analysed in advance for its security relevance as the other language elements. For the approach aimed at facilitating compliance assessment for BPEL-defined business processes based on an analysis of the security relevance of BPEL as a specification language, BPEL scripts containing such extensions have to be excluded since they escape from this approach. It is anticipated, that business processes in a collaborative environment, in general, can avoid the use of such extensions. However, if the requirement for such extensions exists and if it can be assumed that they will be agreed upon between the business partners before using them, the approach proposed here may be adapted to also comprise such extensions. Given particular extensions to be used are known beforehand, they can be subject to an analysis for their security relevance similar the one presented in Chapter 4 for the standardised language elements. After that, the methods deduced from this analysis as described in the following chapters may be adapted accordingly to also accommodate such pre-defined extensions. However, dealing with such extensions in BPEL scripts is expected to increase complexity of the assessment procedure and may be particularly difficult to be incorporated in automatic compliance assessment. For the considerations on security relevance of BPEL in this book, scripts containing extensions have been excluded.

4.3 Classification of Security Policy-Derived Restrictions for WS Invocation

As discussed above, the language constructs will be investigated in conjunction with different types of Web services because in BPEL scripts access to information or resources may only be gained via Web services. Given a particular set of restrictions implied by a security policy that is associated to a particular set of privileges (*i.e.*, a particular role), Web services may be distinguished with respect to access allowance or restrictions to their input and output parameters. Table 1 shows six different classes of access restrictions to Web services as a whole or to Web service parameters that will be considered in the analysis of security relevance of BPEL. There are additional access restrictions derived from security policy rules that are not covered by these six classes. Reasons for not including them into Table 1 for consideration in this analysis will be given during the discussion in this chapter.

The classes 1 and 2 relate to Web services as a whole while classes 3 through 6 relate to the input and output parameters of Web services. Obviously, class 1 denoting Web services with unrestricted access to all resources and information offered by them does not represent an actual restriction category (since no restriction applies at all), but is added here for completeness of this classification. Class 2 represents the opposite of class 1, Web services that are disallowed to be invoked at all whatever parts of their resources or information would be concerned.

The restrictions in class 3 relate to output parameters of a Web service invocation and denote the restriction that information provided by those parameter to the invoking party are not allowed to be carried to particular destinations. Following the simplification rules stated in Section 4.1.4, this type of restriction is meant to denote information flow restriction from the domain executing a business process to any destination outside this domain. In order to allow for more flexibility, when applied to an output parameter of a Web service this restriction can be amended by a relaxation statement indicating one or several external destinations to which information flow will be allowed despite this restriction.

Table 1: Classification of Access Restrictions to Web Services and WS Parameters

Classes	Description
1	Web service with unrestricted access to all parts of resources or information offered
2	Web service with completely restricted access (*i.e.*, Web service that is not allowed to be invoked)
3	Output parameter of a Web service with restricted visibility of values returned (*i.e.*, restriction with respect to forward information flow): Some information made accessible is not allowed to be carried outside the executing domain (*i.e.*, parameter returned is only allowed to be used within the executing domain, but not in outbound messages to targets outside this domain). Some relaxation of this restriction to dedicated targets may apply as explicitly indicated.
4	Optional input parameter of a Web service with usage restrictions (in two alternate versions): a) optional parameter is not allowed to be used at all b) optional parameter always has to be passed to avoid default definition for this parameter to take effect
5	Input parameter of a Web service with constrained set of values allowed: input parameter may only be used with particular values being a subset of the values allowed by the syntactic definition of this parameter
6	Input parameter of a Web service with values restricted to specific sources: only values from particular sources may be used, for instance, only values returned by a particular Web service or a particular Web service parameter

The restriction classes 4 through 6 relate to input parameters of a Web service. Class 4 denotes the restrictions with respect to the use of optional parameters. Despite the definition of a Web service parameter as being optional, security policy can require that such a parameter is not allowed to be used or, contrary, has to be used in any invocation of the particular Web service. Reason for prohibited use of an optional parameter could be that the security policy-derived rules applicable for the particular role would prevent an input parameter to be used because it would offer access to resources or information that is not allowed to be used by this role. For instance, in the CBP example of Figure 4, an optional input parameter to Web service checkStock could effectuate a preferential treatment of the order. In case this functionality would not be made accessible to a business process remotely defined by the car manufacturer, this parameter would be disallowed to be used by a BPEL script imported from the car manufacturer.

As another case of class 4 restrictions, it could be required that an optional input parameter is required to be used in every invocation of the particular Web service. An example of such a restriction in the business process of Figure 4 could be that an optional parameter of Web service calculateOffer would indicate the amount of rebate offered to the client. In case that this optional parameter has a default value indicating a rebate level that will not be offered to the car manufacturer, restriction rules would require that this parameter would be passed with every invocation from a business process defined by the car manufacturer and that its value lies in a certain range. This example reveals that requiring an optional parameter to be present in a Web service invocation often results in an additional restriction of class 5 or 6 (see below).

Restrictions of class 5 require that only values from a particular set of allowed values be used for the respective input parameters of a Web service. Obviously, this restricted set of allowed values will be a subset of the syntactic allowed values of the particular parameter. An example for this kind of restrictions in the CBP of Figure 4 could be that an input parameter of the calculateOffer Web service could indicate the level of rebate provided for in calculating the offer. If the syntax of this parameter would be defined to take on values from the range 5%–50%, but for the car manufacturer only rebates in the range of 5%–30% are offered, then this input parameter would be constrained to the value range [5%–30%] though the syntax of the parameter would allow values in the range [5%–50%]. It should be noted, though this kind of restriction looks like a syntactic one, it actually represents a restriction with respect to the semantics of this parameter since the syntax of the parameter being defined to adopt values in the range [5%–50%] and being checked by a parser in the executing platform would not be changed because of this security policy induced constraint of the value range. Therefore, this restriction cannot be considered a syntactic one because the parameter still is capable to accept values in the range [5%–50%].

Class 6 denotes restrictions with respect to the source of values that are allowed to be passed to an input parameter of a Web service. This kind of restriction does not impose any constraint to input parameters with respect to allowed values but only requires that values passed to these input parameters are restricted to only come from particular sources. In business process context, such sources usually are output parameters of previous Web service invocations.

As can be easily seen, Web services with unrestricted access permission (class 1) as well as Web services with total access restriction (class 2) do not pose any particular challenge for analysis. With these classes, any further distinction between combinations with different activities of BPEL is not relevant. The reason for this is that their allowed or forbidden use in a BPEL script may already be detected by examining the declaration part. No Web service with total access restriction (class 2) must occur in the declaration part, or at least, if such a Web service should occur in the declaration part, it must not be used in any message exchange performed in the business process. Conversely, Web services with unrestricted access permission (class 1) may be invoked freely throughout a business process, irrespective of particular combinations with BPEL activities. The only aspect relevant with Web services of class 1 is the information flow to and from parameters of such a Web service prior and succeeding its invocation, respectively. Any value passed to input parameters of such a Web service must obey possible information flow restrictions of class 3 imposed to output parameters of other Web services. Equally, any value returned by an output parameter of such a Web service is required to observe the restrictions of class 5 and 6 imposed to Web service invocations in the further course of the business process.

The distinction between classes 3 through 6 requires detailed knowledge of the semantics of a Web service. Since such detailed knowledge of external Web services may not be available in the executing domain, external Web services, in general, tend to fall into classes 1 or 2. Conversely, the semantics of internal Web services can be assumed to be well-known within the executing domain such that the differentiation between classes 3 through 6 will be possible.

There is another distinguishable aspect in Web service invocation. This distinction differentiates between Web services accessible independent from the location of the invoker or Web services only allowed to be accessed from inside the executing domain, but not from inside the remote domain defining the BPEL script. For Web services of the executing domain, the latter may be very common since this usually is the reason for bringing the BPEL script from the remote domain to the executing domain. If all Web services invoked would be accessible independent of the location of the invoker, there would be no obvious reason for not running the script in the domain where it is defined with the possible exception that enabling cross-domain invocation would pose problems in the lower layers responsible for access control (*e.g.*, problems with appropriately redefinition of firewall rules to just allow remote access to particular Web services from one particular external domain but still preventing such access from other domains).

Since the location-dependent allowance for invoking a Web service is nothing special for local Web services in the executing domain (*e.g.*, domain B in the example of Figure 4), this situation needs no special observation. However, there may also be external Web services, for example the Web services priceQuotation in domain C in Figure 4, that are only allowed to be invoked from inside the executing domain B, but not from inside domain A. In fact, for purposes of the analysis in this section, it has to be determined whether the semantics of the external Web services are known to an extent that allows for classification into classes 1 through 6 above. If this is not the case, such Web services have to be treated as belonging to class 1, because classification of its parameters into classes different from class 1 is not possible due to lack of knowledge about their semantics.

If only Web services with unrestricted accessibility occur (class 1), the business process could also be executed at the domain where it is specified (with the possible exception relating to accessibility mentioned above). The only difference in having such a business process executed in a different domain is the fact, that computational and communicational load involved is moved to this other domain. With respect to security, this is only relevant as bearing the potential for making exhaustive use of computational or communicational resources of this other domain. If driven to an extreme, this could cause a form of denial of service attack in this domain. As such exceptional behaviour may easily be controlled by the runtime environment executing the BPEL script, this is not considered to constitute a security threat in this context that needs particular examination before running a BPEL script. However, detecting such behaviour by analysing the BPEL script prior to execution is also feasible. This aspect, although neglectable in a CBP context, may require further consideration in other contexts where appropriate measures to prevent exaggerated usage of resources cannot be anticipated. A further discussion on this aspect will take place in Chapter 8.

4.4   Analysis of Security-Relevant Semantic Patterns of BPEL

In this section, the building blocks of BPEL-definable semantics of a business process that are used for the purposes of the security analysis are identified and the results of this analysis are presented.

4.4.1   Definition of Security-Relevant Semantic Patterns of BPEL

To determine their relevance with respect to security policies, in particular access control and information flow control, combinations of information passed to or received from Web services associated with restrictions belonging to the classes of Table 1 with the activities defined in BPEL are investigated. These combinations are denoted security-relevant semantic patterns in this book and considered appropriate building blocks of BPEL-definable business process semantics for the purposes of analysis of the security relevance of BPEL as a specification language. It should be noted that the term "semantic pattern" is used by other authors differently[133]. We also use the term "semantic pattern" here as an abbreviation for the

---

133   *e.g.*, Staab *et. al.*, 2000, Hao *et. al.*, 2008

complete term "security-relevant semantic patterns", but only if the relation to security relevance is obvious from the context.

When activities are directly concerned with Web service invocation or message exchange with partners, the meaning of such combinations is obvious. Combinations with activities not directly concerned with Web service invocation need further explanation. Combining a parameter subject to a restriction of a certain class and a particular BPEL activity denotes the situation where the information passed to or returned by such a parameter has been or will be used in combination with this type of activity. Of course, a particular Web service parameter may belong to more than one of the classes 3 through 6 simultaneously. For the ease of discussion, no combined classes are analysed, since for a Web service parameter belonging to more than one of these classes, the results related to each of the classes it belongs to may be applied simultaneously in this situation.

4.4.2 Results of Security Analysis of Semantic Patterns

As already mentioned in Section 4.3, security-relevant semantic patterns involving access restrictions of classes 1 and 2 need no further investigation. The results of the analysis of these semantic patterns involving information flow restrictions of classes 3 through 6 are depicted in Tables 2 and 3 and discussed in this section. While Table 2 presents the results for security-relevant semantic patterns formed by combination with primitive activities, Table 3 indicates the results for structured activities.

Tables 2 and 3 each comprise five columns. The second column contains a short description of the semantics of the respective BPEL activity in the first column. In columns three through five, the implications for security assessment are indicated, when the respective BPEL activity is combined with information exchanged with a Web service subject to restrictions of classes 3 through 6. Since the entries for classes 5 and 6 only differ slightly, the indications for these classes are combined in the fifth column.

An entry of "–" indicates that the respective semantic pattern is not relevant in scope of access control and information flow. As shown in Tables 2 and 3, some semantic patterns require special attention with respect to information flow indicated by entry IFA followed by a parenthesised letter. The meanings of the different variants of this type are as follows: An entry IFA(v) denotes the requirement of forward information flow analysis with respect to information returned by Web service parameters subject to class 3 restrictions. The entry IFA(r) denotes the requirement for backward information flow analysis with respect to Web service parameters subject to class 5 restriction (*i.e.*, restricted value range) and entry IFA(s)) denotes the requirement for backward information flow analysis with respect to Web service parameters subject to class 6 restriction (*i.e.*, restricted source of values passed to these parameters).

Security patterns involving class 3 restricted information and one of the activities
invoke (with respect to the inbound parameters, *i.e.*, the output parameters of the
Web service invoked), receive or the on message part of pick (in the latter cases
with respect to the inbound parameters of a message received from a partner) are
security-relevant since information received from these activities may cause security policy violations when passed to targets outside the executing domain (except
those targets were indicated explicitly as exceptions from the general visibility
restriction). As can be seen in Table 2, information flow analysis in forward direction is required to determine whether visibility-restricted information returned by
the Web service is kept inside the security domain and is not sent outside via one
of the activities invoke (within an outbound parameter) or reply unless the target
is indicated explicitly as allowed within the exceptions to the particular information flow restriction.

Table 2: Security Relevance of Semantic Patterns with Primitive Activities

Primitive Activities		Class 3	Class 4	Cl. 5/6
invoke	Invocation of a Web service	IFA(v)	u	IFA(r/s)
receive	Waiting for a message to arrive	IFA(v)	–	–
reply	Sending a reply to a message received	–	u	IFA(r/s)
assign	Assignment of values between two different locations (see note)	(relevant in IFA only)		
wait	Waiting for a specified amount of time	time(v)	–	–
throw	Indication of exceptions such as failures during execution	except(v)	–	–
rethrow*	Forwarding of exceptions causing fault handler execution to contai-ning scope	–	–	–
empty	No operation	–	–	–
validate	Validate values against type decla-ration of variable	val(v)	–	–
exit	Termination of a process instance	exit(v)	–	–
compensate*	Initiate compensation as specified by compensation handlers of cor-responding scope and all nested scopes	–	–	–
compensate Scope*	Initiate compensation of activities as specified by compensation handler of a specific scope	scope(v)	–	–

Note: For attribute **validate** possibly contained in this activity see discussion below on activity **validate**.

*	=	Activity only to be used within fault handlers
−	=	Not relevant for access control and information flow
u	=	Check that actual use complies to usage restriction of optional WS parameter
IFA	=	Information flow analysis,
		(v) with respect to visibility of values returned from WS,
		(r) with respect to ranges of values passed to WS,
		(s) with respect to sources of values passed to WS

For class 4, only `invoke` (with respect to the outbound parameters, *i.e.*, the input parameters of the Web service invoked) and `reply` need special attention to check that the restricted input parameters of the Web service or the output parameter in a message sent to a partner will be used conforming to the particular usage restriction indicated by entry u (*i.e.*, not used or always present depending on the embodiment of this restriction). Classes 5 and 6 are similar, since with `invoke` (with respect to the outbound parameters) and `reply` information flow analysis is required to determine whether the restricted use of values is obeyed. With class 5, backward information flow analysis related to the values written to restricted outbound parameters is required (indicated by entry IFA(r), whereas with class 6, analysis is required with respect to the sources of such values (indicated by entry IFA(s)).

As indicated in Table 2, analysis of information flow has to embrace `assign` activities to observe the movement of information within the business process. If processing such as calculation or string manipulation is performed within a BPEL script using language constructs imported from, for instance, XPath[134], it has to be analysed that no restricted information is involved, or at least, that results from the processing is not used in a manner violating the security policies. Since allowing such kind of processing on restricted information could cause obfuscation of information flow, thereby complicating the analysis of information flow, as a matter of precaution such processing should be generally considered incompatible with security policy, independent of the further use of its results. Since it can be assumed that any such processing will be performed in Web services invoked by a business process such that no need for any such processing exists within the process itself, for the purpose of our considerations, incorporation of any elements from XPath or other XML specifications providing data manipulation such as XQuery[135] or XSLT[136] has been excluded.

The activities `empty`, `compensate`, and `rethrow` involve no security relevance whatsoever. This is quite obvious for the `empty` activity. For the `compensate` activity, this can be seen by the consideration that this activity only initiates compensation from within a fault handler but, by its own, has no effect with respect to

---

134 Berglund *et al.*, 2006
135 Boag *et al.*, 2007
136 Kay, 2007

observable behaviour of the business process. The business logic performed in the course of compensation is specified by activities in the respective compensation handlers. The security relevance of these activities is subject to separate examination of the compensation handlers and the outcome of this examination is not associated with the activity initiating these handlers to be executed. Also for the `re-throw` activity, the reason for not being security-relevant relates to the fact that this activity simply forwards the exception that caused the fault handler containing this activity to be executed to the environment of this fault handler that is the scope at the next higher nesting level or the process level. Since passing of information stays within the process being executed, and the exception to be passed is predetermined without any choice for passing different information, no risk for violation of information flow restrictions exist.

However, the `compensateScope` activity which is quite similar to `compensate` bears security relevance of its own. Reason for this is that this activity selects one particular compensation handler for execution. If this selection would depend on visibility-restricted information, the fact that this particularly selected compensation took place could be observed from outside to conclude on the value of the class 3 information and thereby could be exploited to establish a covert channel for information leakage.

Similarly, use of visibility-restricted information gained from Web services of class 3 in the activities `wait` (with respect to duration), `throw` (with respect to exception thrown and information passed along with exception), `exit` (with respect to condition for termination), `if` (with respect to definition of alternate flows), `while` and `repeatUntil` (both with respect to loop control), `forEach` (with respect to loop boundaries as well as to conditions for pre-emptive termination of iteration), and `pick` (with respect to timeout interval) also turn out to be security-relevant as shown in Tables 2 and 3 because of the risk of establishing covert channels. Defining any of the terms indicated in parenthesis with the above activities dependent on visibility-restricted information could be exploited to circumvent restrictions implied by security policy. For instance, if the visibility-restricted information *I* is used to control the amount of loop cycles in a `while` activity, providing some externally observable behaviour such as sending a message to an external Web service from within the loop body could be used to circumvent the visibility restriction on *I*. In this way, an external observer would be able to count the numbers of such messages and deduce the value of *I* from this observation. However, revealing *I* to an external observer would violate the security policy restricting this information from being disclosed outside the domain.

With respect to potential covert channels, also the activity `validate` as well as the attribute `validate` of the `assign` activity require special attention. If variables declared within a BPEL script containing visibility-restricted information are to be validated, possible value range restrictions specified in their types' definition could leak information contradicting security policy implied information flow restrictions. Consider, for example, a variable `receivePriceInfo` declared to be of a fictitious type `belowThousand` which has been derived from the simple XML-type `integer` with the additional restriction `xsd:maxInclusive value= "999"`. If this variable would be used to store the visibility-restricted output parameter `price` returned from a Web service invocation (*e.g.*, an inquiry similar to Web service `priceQuotation` in Figure 4 indicating the price of a single item), then validation of this variable after storing the price would leak information about the price via externally observable behaviour of the business process. The negative outcome of this validation would cause a standard `bpel:invalidVariables` fault to be thrown. An observer who has written the BPEL script and sent it to the executing domain for performing the business process corresponding to this script would know that the price returned from this Web service was greater than or equal to 1000 when this exception would occur and that the price was less than 1000 when no exception occurs. Obviously, by cascading of validations against varying types, visibility-restricted information could be propagated to an arbitrary level of detail by causing or avoiding `bpel:invalidVariables` faults in `validate` activities.

Table 3: Security Relevance of Semantic Patterns with Structured Activities

Structured Activities		Class 3	Class 4	Classes 5/6
sequence	Definition of a fixed execution order	–	–	–
flow	Parallel execution of activities	–	–	–
If	Branching between several alternate activities depending on conditions	branch cond(v)	–	–
while	Iterative execution, *i.e.*, looping	loop cond(v)	–	–
repeat Until				
forEach	Iterative consecutive or parallel execution	iteration bounds(v) preempt(v)	–	–
pick	Waiting simultaneously for several events to occur and proceeding with the first event that actually occurs (see note)	IFA(v) time(v)	– –	– –

Note: Typically, one of the events waited for is a timeout event, while the other events are messages to arrive

–   = Not relevant for access control and information flow

IFA(v) = Information flow analysis with respect to visibility of values returned from WS

The additional flow control and structuring elements of BPEL as introduced in Section 4.2.3 are not included in Tables 2 and 3 because they are not considered activities. The additional flow control via links in `target` and `source` elements of activities within a `flow` activity expose security relevance as indicated above with `while` or `if` activities if their flow control mechanisms are made dependent on information flow restricted information (class 3 restriction) thereby bearing the risk of establishing a covert channel. The Boolean expressions contained in a `join-Condition` with element `target`, and in a `transitionCondition` with ele-ment `source`, must not depend on any visibility-restricted information in order to avoid covert channels with these constructs.

From the additional structuring elements of BPEL, event handlers contribute additional security-relevant semantics as will be discussed below. The other structuring elements, that are scopes, fault handlers, compensation handlers and termination handlers, do not provide any security-relevant semantics on their own. Of course, the activities contained in all of these handlers exhibit the same security relevance as if they were used in the definition of the main stream of a business process. Nevertheless, these structuring elements need to be observed during compliance assessment of particular BPEL scripts since they provide particular execution semantics to the activities contained in them. Fault handlers as well as compensation handlers that can be linked to the execution path of fault handlers via the compensation activities represent process logic to be executed in the case of exceptions or errors, collectively denoted as faults. Since such faults may happen at virtually any time during process execution these fault handlers and the compensation handlers eventually initiated by them can be thought of as potential flows parallel to the main processing flow of the process and, therefore, have to be treated as such during information flow analysis.

In contrast, event handlers contribute to the security-relevant semantics of BPEL in that they specify possible interaction with the environment of the business process. The `onEvent` and `onAlarm` elements contained in such handlers taken together exhibit similar semantics as a `pick` activity. The `onEvent` elements of event handlers like the `onMessage` elements of a `pick` activity work like a `receive` activity, that is they wait for messages to arrive on partner links. Therefore, these elements represent security-relevant semantics if information flow-restricted information (class 3 restriction) is received this way and information flow analysis in forward direction is required in this case to verify that such information is only used in a way conforming to these restrictions. Furthermore, in the same way as the `onAlarm` elements of a `pick` activity, these elements provide the capability of establishing covert channels if the duration of such a timeout surveillance is made dependent on visibility-restricted information.

Though very similar to a `pick` activity, there is a significant difference between event handlers and this activity. While a `pick` activity blocks further processing in its flow until one of the messages waited for has arrived or a timeout occurred, event handlers do not block normal processing but wait for the messages or timeout events in parallel to normal process flow. Furthermore, if one of the messages specified in event handlers arrives or a specified timeout occurs, this waiting for messages or timeout events is not terminated as in the case of a `pick` activity but remains active until the containing scope or the process as a whole (in the case of event handlers specified at process level) terminates. For information flow purposes, event handlers may be thought of as a `pick` activity contained in a endless loop (`while` activity with Boolean constant true as looping condition) that executes parallel to the activity specified in a scope or parallel to the activity specified at process level, that is contained in a `flow` activity together with this scope-level or process-level activity. From this consideration it becomes clear how event handlers have to be treated during information flow analysis during security policy assessment of a BPEL script containing such handlers.

4.5 Considerations with Respect to Separation of Duty Constraints

In addition to the security policy-derived restrictions to Web service invocation from within a business process discussed in Section 4.3, there is another type of restriction derived from security policies not considered in this analysis. This type of restriction is known as separation of duty (SoD) and well-studied in literature[137]. Restrictions of this type are either static or dynamic. The static version demands that multiple roles of a particular set of roles cannot be adopted by the same principal (user) over time (*i.e.*, once a principal has adopted one role he will never adopt any further role of the same set). Applying such constraints to Web service invocations implies that different Web services requiring access privileges associated with different roles in such a set cannot be invoked by the same principal. With respect to business processes, this means that the same process is not allowed to invoke Web services belonging to different sets of access privileges constrained by so-called static SoD policies.

The other form of SoD, called dynamic SoD, is a relaxation of the static variant in that it allows the same principal to adopt different roles subject to SoD constraints, but not at the same time or not in the same operational context. It should be noted that these alternate dynamic conditions sometimes are treated as separate subtypes of dynamic SoD[138]. The typical example for this type of constraint is a payment process where the issuer of a payment order is not allowed to release or authorise the same order while he may well be allowed to release a payment not initiated by himself. In the context of Web services and business processes, enforcement of dynamic SoD constraints is based on the history of Web services invoked and instances of business objects handled.

---

137 Wijesekera and Jajodia, 2003; Schaad and Moffett, 2002, Schaad *et al.*, 2006, Ribeiro *et al.*, 2001; Strembeck and Mendling, 2011

138 Schaad and Moffett, 2002, pp. 19, 20

While static SoD constraints may be enforced at business process level by not invoking Web services associated to conflicting privileges in the same process, controlling the obedience of dynamic SoD constraints in business processes based on mechanisms provided by BPEL seems to be difficult or even impossible. Reasons for this are the lack of information and the lack of influence on who is going to invoke the Web service offered by a business process. Remember that BPEL does not offer any mechanisms for access control. This difficulty exists independently of whether the process has been defined locally or remotely. Approaches to cover dynamic SoD requirements not necessarily specific to business processes or Web services exist[139]. Obviously, enforcement of dynamic SoD constraints requires mechanisms applied at runtime.

Since the approach presented in this book is mainly based on static analysis of business process semantics, it is not claimed that this approach will be appropriate to contribute to enforcement of dynamic SoD requirements. However, static SoD constraints may be adequately addressed in this approach. A discussion of this and some sort of workaround for dynamic SoD constraints are contained in Chapter 5.

4.6 Summary

In this chapter, the results of analysing BPEL as a specification language for its security-relevant semantics have been presented. In order to aim for universal results not bound to particular examples of BPEL scripts or application contexts in which business processes are defined, preferably small building blocks of BPEL-definable business process semantics enabling sensible observations with respect to security relevance were searched for. Combinations of BPEL activities with policy-induced restrictions to Web service invocations have turned out to be suitable for that purpose. These combinations were referred to as security-relevant semantic patterns of BPEL. Such a pattern may be thought of passing information sent or received in messages exchanged with Web services or invokers of the business process (i.e., invokers of the Web service provided by the business process) and being subject to certain access or information flow restrictions through a particular language construct of BPEL.

For the purpose of this analysis, security policy derived restrictions to be obeyed at business process layer (and not already dealt with by security mechanisms provided in layers below the business process layer) when considering CBPs in a business-to-business context have been categorised. Investigation of their security relevance when combined with the different BPEL activities leads to requirements for information flow analysis to be performed when assessing a BPEL-defined business process for compliance with security policy.

---

139 *e.g.,* Schaad and Moffett, 2002; Botha and Eloff, 2001; Strembeck and Mendling, 2011

The results of the analysis of security-relevant semantics of BPEL-defined business processes, as described in this section, have been published as a conference paper[140], with an extended version being presented in a related journal paper[141].

Based on these results concerning the security relevance of the semantic patterns, a formalism was defined to specify existing security policies in such a way that checking BPEL scripts for compliance with these policies will be facilitated considerably. How this formalism was established and how security assessment can benefit from this formalism, will be discussed in the next chapter.

---

140 Fischer *et al.*, 2006
141 Fischer *et al.*, 2007b

5 Specification of Security Policy for Compliance Assessment of CBPs

The analysis of BPEL as a specification language in the former chapter has revealed the potential of violating security policy-implied restrictions to Web service invocation, in particular with respect to information flow of values passed to and returned from Web services. From the outset, one major aim was to define methods that support assessment of remotely defined business processes for compliance with security policies in force at the location of execution. This chapter introduces novel approaches to security policy enforcement based on the results presented in Chapter 4.

The methods proposed herein for facilitating this compliance assessment were inspired by concepts developed in conformance testing methodology of open systems as defined in a series of International Standards (CTMF, Conformance Testing Methodology and Framework, ISO/IEC 9646, part 1–7; particularly[142]). In this series of International Standards, a so-called Protocol Implementation Conformance Statement proforma (PICS proforma) has been defined for the following purpose: Having defined a (standardised) test suite for conformance testing of implementations claiming to comply to a specific communication protocol in the OSI protocol stack, the problem occurs that this test suite has to be adapted before testing a particular implementation. Given the variety of implementation options provided by those OSI protocol specifications, it has to be assured that only such functionality an implementation claims to support will be subject to conformance testing. Therefore, the PICS proforma which is specific to a particular OSI protocol specification provides a checklist to be filled in by the implementing side to indicate which options provided by the protocol specification for implementation choice has been actually chosen and which alternatives have been adopted. Submitting this filled-in PICS proforma to a test centre as a first step during conformance assessment enables the test centre to perform a static analysis of the choices taken for the implementation in order to assess that this particular set of choices is conformant to the standard in question. For instance, a standard may require that a particular choice of an option A may only be allowed if a choice of a related option B is made in a specific manner (e.g., support both options or none of them). After checking a PICS proforma for conformant choices of options, the test centre will be able to adapt the test suite to be used during conformance testing of the particular protocol implementation to the indications made in this proforma. For example, if a PICS proforma for an implementation under test (IUT) would state that the

---

142 ISO, 1994

optional functionality F1 is not supported by the current implementation and the test centre has already verified that this was in accordance with the standard, then the test suite would be adapted in such a manner that test cases that are to test support of functionality F1 would not be performed during the process of conformance testing for that particular IUT and that the non-support of this functionality would be consistent throughout the implementation. For instance, refusing to support optional functionality F1 in one context (*e.g.*, during connection establishment), but supporting the same functionality F1 in another context (*e.g.*, during data transmission) would usually result in a fail verdict of the conformance test assessment.

This approach of indicating a variable set of implementation options to be used for adapting the type and amount of test cases to be performed during conformance testing of a particular implementation that claims to comply to a protocol standard gave rise to the method proposed in this project in order to support and facilitate the assessment of compliance with security policies for remotely defined BPEL scripts. After analysis of the security-relevant features of BPEL, a checklist comparable to a PICS proforma[143] can be provided, that allows for specification of security policy-derived restrictions to be obeyed during execution of remotely defined BPEL scripts. This way, the security policy of a domain executing remotely defined BPEL scripts is re-specified in order to only contain rules that are relevant at the business process layer in this context. This checklist is called a security policy statement (SPS) proforma or template and will be used to indicate allowed features of BPEL in compliance with the security policy. Unlike with PICS proformas in conformance testing of OSI protocol standards, the roles of filling in and using the filled-in checklist are distributed differently in a compliance assessment of remotely defined BPEL scripts. The SPS proforma will be filled in by the executing domain to indicate the security policy-implied restrictions applicable to such BPEL scripts. A separate SPS proforma will be required to be filled in for each remote domain that is allowed to remotely define BPEL scripts for execution in a particular executing domain. The indications made in a filled-in SPS proforma (simply called SPS in the following) will determine the kind of inspections to be performed during compliance assessment of a BPEL script from the domain indicated in the SPS as originator. A role comparable to that of a test centre in the conformance testing context is taken by the site performing the compliance assessment with security policies.

It should be noted that though the concept of using an SPS proforma to direct the compliance assessment procedure was inspired by experiences from the field of conformance testing of open communication protocols, in other respects the methods proposed herein for compliance assessment expressly are not based on testing techniques but are rather comparable with code inspection techniques. This

---

143 ISO, 1994

distinction matters in particular because testing always requires some sort of execution of the code or script under test but code inspection does not since it may and usually will be performed prior to execution of the object under consideration.

5.1 Redefinition of Security Policy in Terms of Security-Relevant Semantic Patterns

As already indicated in the introduction to this chapter, the security policy is to be re-specified to express the restrictions applicable to remotely defined business processes. This re-specification shall be performed in such a manner that assessing a remotely defined BPEL script for compliance with these restrictions can be performed in an as straightforward as possible way. The results of the analysis of security-relevant semantics of BPEL in the former chapter have shown that such semantics is closely related to restrictions implied by security policies to Web service invocations. Therefore, the idea for re-specifying security policies in order to facilitate compliance assessment is to provide indications of the classified restrictions summarised in Table 1 for all Web services, a remotely defined BPEL script is allowed to invoke. In this way, the assessment process receives its directives what to watch out when assessing a BPEL script. Based on the information contained in an SPS, the assessment process can check whether only allowed Web services are to be invoked in a BPEL script under consideration and that invocations occur in a manner compliant to the restrictions imposed to them by security policies of the executing domain.

As can be seen from Tables 2 and 3 above, most restrictions imposed to Web service invocations with respect to particular input and output parameters imply information flow analysis in forward and backward direction in order to verify that the restrictions are obeyed. Therefore, indications made relating to restriction classes of Web service invocations already provide an outline of the particular checking methods to be applied when a BPEL script is subject to compliance assessment.

5.2 Security Policy Statement

In a security policy statement (SPS), the security policy of one particular domain (*e.g.*, domain B in Figure 2 that is the executing domain) with respect to one particular other domain (*e.g.*, domain A in Figure 2 that is the domain specifying a BPEL script and sending it for remote execution) is expressed in terms of restrictions or allowance of security patterns identified and analysed in Chapter 4. To this end, the internal and external Web services, that are allowed to be invoked by a business process executing in domain B on behalf of domain A will be indicated together with the restrictions applying to their respective input and output parameters. In order to structure the information contained in it, the SPS is composed of several parts each of which containing particulars related to a group of related restrictions, for instance, related to a specific Web service that is allowed to be invoked.

In order to discuss this approach in more detail, an example presenting some typical information contained in an SPS template is shown in Figure 7. The exemplary entries contained in this SPS are taken from the example CBP in Chapter 2.

5.2.1   Security Policy Statement Template

The SPS starts with its main part, called Security Policy Statement Template. In its top part, it comprises information identifying the issuing domain that is the executing domain to which the security policy expressed in the SPS relates (*i.e.*, the domain of the gearbox manufacturer in this example). Furthermore, the application context and the foreign domain to which the restrictions in the SPS relate are identified. Here, this is the application context of processing orders for gearboxes and parts of it for the domain of the car manufacturer sending a BPEL script for execution in domain B.

Security Policy Statement		
For executing domain: *GearBoxManufacturer domainB*		
(possibly additional identifying information not of interest in this example)		
For application Context: *Order management of gear boxes and part of it*		
Relating to BPEL scripts from domain: *CarManufacturer.domainA*		
Invocation of Web services outside current domain allowed?		Y/N: *Y*
If yes, indicate allowed external Web services:		
URI: *priceQuotation.SubSupplier1.domainC1*	Reference to EWSRS	*EWSR1*
URI: *priceQuotation.SubSupplier2.domainC2*	Reference to EWSRS	*EWSR2*
URI: *checkOffer.CarManufacturer.domainA*	Reference to EWSRS	*EWSR3*
Indicate restricted internal Web services:		
URI: *checkStock.domainB*	Reference to IWSRS	*IWSR1*
URI: *calculateOffer.domainB*	Reference to IWSRS	*IWSR2*
URI: *completeOffer.domainB*	Reference to IWSRS	*IWSR3*
Indicate unrestricted internal Web Services:		
URI: *none*		
(Further indications with respect to allowed semantics (e.g., allowed processing on information gained from Web service invocation) may be indicated here)		

Figure 7: Security Policy Statement Template with Exemplary Entries

It should be noted that distinguishing between different application contexts in different SPSs provides the capability to indicate different sets of allowed and disallowed Web service invocations for the same pair of executing domain and defining domain. For example, if the same car manufacturer is also allowed to send BPEL scripts for business processes executed in a context where construction plans for new gearbox models are to be exchanged between the car manufacturer and the gearbox manufacturer and manipulated in cooperation between the development units of both organisations, it can easily be imagined that a totally different set of Web services would be involved and, therefore, a different SPS would apply to this application context even though the same organisations (*i.e.*, the car manufacturer and the gearbox manufacturer) would be involved.

After this identification part, information follows indicating Web services that are allowed to be invoked by a business process defined by and executed on behalf of the foreign domain (domain B in this example). First, there is a general indication as to whether invocation of Web services in foreign domains will be allowed at all or not. If invocation of such Web services is not generally prohibited, there will be indications of particular foreign Web services that are allowed to be invoked each identified by its respective URI. In this example, the respective Web services priceQuotation of the two sub-suppliers C_1 and C_2 as well as the call-back Web service checkOffer of the car manufacturer are foreign Web services allowed to be invoked. For each allowed external Web service, a so-called External Web Service Restriction Statement (EWSRS) will be referenced that contains further information concerning restrictions with respect to the particular Web service. In this example, three external Web services have been indicated. Only those external Web services indicated explicitly in this part of the SPS will be allowed to be invoked by a remotely defined BPEL script from domain A. One could think of some sort of wildcard indication, for example '*' in place of a constituent of an URI, if all Web services of a particular domain or sub-domain are allowed to be invoked. However, since only examples involving a small number of allowed Web services are used in the proof of concept for our approach, the definition of such notational shortcuts is out of scope.

After indication of the allowed external Web services, there are two further groups of indications in Figure 7 relating to Web services of the executing domain: one group relating to internal Web services for which invocation is restricted and one group relating to internal Web services that may be invoked without any restrictions. Remember that the last group corresponds to class 1 of Table 1, albeit only for internal Web services. For the purpose of this study it is supposed that only internal Web services of class 1 actually occur and that all external Web services fall into one of the classes 2 through 6. In cases where unrestricted external Web services actually occur, this could be indicated by omission of the reference to an EWSRS for the particular Web service.

While the last type of entry (*i.e.*, Web service of class 1) does not require any further information besides the URI of the particular Web service, for each restricted internal Web service there is a field indicating a reference to a so-called Internal Web Service Restriction Statement (IWSRS) similar to the indication for external Web services above. In this example, the three internal Web services of the gearbox manufacturer depicted in Figure 4 are indicated as allowed internal Web services with restrictions. Both the group of EWSRS and the group of IWSRS referenced in Figure 7 are considered part of the SPS as a whole.

The SPS is understood to indicate all of the security-relevant semantics in a BPEL script from the specific foreign domain (domain A in this example) acceptable for cross-domain deployment. Therefore, all other security-relevant semantics not explicitly stated in an SPS as being allowed, will be prohibited. In particular, only the Web services explicitly stated in this part of the SPS will be allowed for invocation in a BPEL script from domain A. It should be noted that Web services with class 2 restriction (*i.e.*, Web services that are not allowed to be invoked at all) will never occur in an SPS.

At the bottom of the SPS template, there is left room for further indications with respect to allowed semantics in a BPEL script from the particular defining domain. Such indications may include allowed processing to be performed on information returned by Web services invoked. As discussed above, BPEL does not provide any means for any kind of data manipulation (besides assignment from one location to another location). Should there be a requirement to perform data processing within a BPEL script, language elements of other XML-based specifications have to be imported. Usually, XQuery[144], XSLT[145], or XPath[146] will be used for such purposes of data processing in BPEL scripts. In the approach presented here, performing data processing in a BPEL-defined business process is supposed to always be achieved by Web service invocation such that import of elements of XPath (or similar specifications) is not required. Thereby, considerations with respect to the security relevance of performing data processing within the BPEL script could be avoided. Note that it is always possible to define a Web service to perform a particular data processing (though it may sometimes be more convenient to perform it directly within the BPEL script). Therefore, this assumption made here does not restrict general applicability of the approach proposed in this book.

5.2.2 Internal Web Service Restriction Statement

In Figure 8, there is an example of an IWSRS template in order to clarify the typical information contained in this part of an SPS. The example relates to the checkStock Web service of the gearbox manufacturer. In this template, there is room for indicating security policy-induced restrictions of any kind that relates to the input and output parameters of the particular Web service. In the heading of this template, the identifier of the IWSRS used for referencing it in the main part of the SPS is indicated. Further, the URI for invoking the particular Web service and the URI of the WSDL definition of this Web service are given.

---

144 Boag *et al.*, 2007
145 Kay, 2007
146 Berglund *et al.*, 2006

Restrictions relating to Web service parameters are those of the classes 3 through 6 in Table 1 above. The indications are grouped by restriction classes starting with the restrictions to input parameters. For class 4 restrictions that always relate to optional input parameters indications may be made whether the particular parameter is prohibited to be used or always required in order to avoid default mechanisms defined for this parameter to be applied. For class 5 restrictions, the input parameters along with the respective allowed values or range of values are to be indicated here. Similarly, for class 6 restrictions, the input parameters along with the respective allowed sources of values passed to these parameters are to be indicated. Such sources may be other Web services or particular output parameters of other Web services.

For the output parameters of a Web service, only class 3 restrictions apply. For every restricted output parameter, a target relaxation may be indicated. While class 3 restricted output parameters are generally allowed to be passed freely to domain-internal Web services (this was anticipated in Section 4.1.4), the values returned by those parameters are restricted to be carried to any external Web service or passed as message or part of a message sent back to the invoker of the business process in a `reply` activity. If there are any exceptions to this restriction, they may be indicated in a separate column by specifying possible external targets (Web services or particular parameters of Web services) to which a visibility-restricted value may exceptionally be passed while still being restricted from passing to all other external target. This type of relaxation for visibility-restricted information is called target relaxation in Figure 8 and the following parts of the book.

Internal Web Service Restriction Statement		IWSRS-ID	*IWSR1*
URI for invocation: *checkStock.domainB*			
URI of WSDL: *wsdl.checkStock.domainB*			
Restrictions with respect to input parameters			
Usage restrictions of optional parameters			
Parameter: *ListOfItems*　　　(indicate 'required' or 'forbidden'	*required*		
Value range restrictions	Allowed values or value ranges:		
Parameter: *ProcessingPriority*	*Prio1, Prio2*		
Restrictions related to sources of values	Allowed source(s) of values:		
Parameter: *none*	–		
Restrictions with respect to output parameters	Target relaxation:		
Parameter: *ListOfItemsToOrderFromSubSupplier1*	*C1.priceQuotation.list*		
Parameter: *AccessCredentialForSubSupplier1*	*C1.priceQuotation.credential*		
Parameter: *ListOfItemsToOrderFromSubSupplier2*	*C2.priceQuotation.list*		
Parameter: *AccessCredentialForSubSupplier2*	*C2.priceQuotation.credential*		

Figure 8: Example of Internal Web Service Restriction Statement

In the case of the checkStock Web service of Figure 4, the input parameter passing the list of items to be ordered is supposed to be an optional parameter for exemplary purposes only. In practice, it may not be particularly sensible to have this parameter as an optional input parameter. In the IWSRS of Figure 8, however, though being defined as an optional parameter, the *ListOfItems* input parameter is indicated as required when this Web service is invoked in a BPEL script from the car manufacturer. Also for the purpose of this example, a parameter controlling the priority of order processing is anticipated. Suppose that this parameter is capable of adopting one of the values in the set {Prio1, Prio2, Prio3} where Prio1 indicates the lowest and Prio3 the highest priority. The IWSRS in Figure 8 indicates that business processes specified by the car manufacturer for controlling the order processing in domain B are restricted to the two lowest priority levels while the highest priority level of order processing is not allowed to be used. Source-restricted input parameters (class 6 restrictions) are not present in this example.

With respect to the output parameters of this Web service, several restrictions apply. As discussed in Section 2.2, the checkStock Web service is supposed to possibly return two lists of items that are found to be out of stock and, therefore, have to be ordered from the two sub-suppliers. Along with the respective list of items to be ordered, the Web service returns a credential required to access the respective Web service priceQuotation. These two pairs of output parameters intended to be passed to sub-supplier 1 and sub-supplier 2, respectively, are visibility-restricted since they are not allowed to be carried outside the domain of the gearbox manufacturer except to the respective Web service of the two sub-suppliers. Therefore, in the IWSRS example it is indicated that the list of items to be ordered from sub-supplier 1 though declared as visibility-restricted is allowed to be passed to the input parameter list of Web service priceQuotation of sub-supplier 1. Similarly, the credentials required to be granted access to this Web service from within the domain B are also declared as visibility-restricted with a target relaxation to the input parameter credential of Web service priceQuotation of sub-supplier 1. In an analogue manner, the output parameters of Web service checkStock intended for sub-supplier 2 are indicated as visibility-restricted in the IWSRS with target relaxations to the respective input parameters of Web service priceQuotation of sub-supplier 2.

5.2.3 External Web Service Restriction Statement

In Figure 9, an example of an EWSRS is shown in order to clarify the typical information contained in this part of an SPS. The content of an EWSRS is quite similar to an IWSRS discussed in the previous section. Both templates differ in the indication whether values of output parameters of the external Web service are allowed to be assigned to input parameters of internal Web services. Such assignments may be prohibited as a matter of precaution in cases where the nature of output values returned by an external Web service is to a large extent unknown at the domain issuing the SPS and, therefore, should not be used as input parameters in invocations of internal Web services. If this restriction applies, the values returned by such an external Web service, unless they are visibility-restricted, may still be used for flow control purposes within the BPEL script or may be passed as input parameters to other external Web services, preferably in the same domain as the Web service addressed by the current EWSRS.

The example EWSRS in Figure 9 relates to the external Web service priceQuotation of sub-supplier 1 from the CBP example in Figure 4. The Web service is supposed to take two input parameters, list and credential. The input parameter list accepts the list of items inquired while the input parameter credential receives the credential required for granting access to this Web service. As can be seen in Figure 9, the input parameter credential has simultaneously two kinds of restrictions, namely a usage restriction (class 4) and a source restriction (class 6). This means that though this input parameter has been defined to be optional, this parameter is required when used within a BPEL script from the car manufacturer and the input value has to be equal to the value of the output parameter AccessCredentialForSubSupplier1 returned by Web service checkStock. Also for the second input parameter of the priceQuotation Web service, a restriction applies with respect to sources of the values passed to it. The value passed has to be the value of output parameter ListOfItemsToOrderFromSubSupplier1 returned by Web service checkStock.

External Web Service Restriction Statement		**EWSRS-ID**	*EWSR1*
URI for invocation: *priceQuotation.domainC1*			
URI of WSDL: *wsdl.priceQuotation.domainC1*			
Restrictions with respect to input parameters			
Usage restrictions of optional parameters			
Parameter: *credential* (indicate 'required' or 'forbidden'		*required*	
Value range restrictions	Allowed values or value range:		
Parameter: *none*	–		
Restrictions related to sources of values	Allowed source(s) of values:		
Parameter: *list*	*B.checkStock.ListOfItemsToOrder FromSubSupplier1*		
Parameter: *credential*	*B.checkStock.AccessCredentialFor SubSupplier1*		
Restrictions with respect to output parameters	Target relaxation:		
Parameter: *priceDeliveryInformation*	*B.calculateOffer.infoSupplier1*		
Assignment of output values to internal Web services allowed?		Y/N: *Y*	

Figure 9: Example of External Web Service Restriction Statement

The only output parameter of this Web service is visibility-restricted. In the case of an external Web service, such a restriction includes internal Web services of the invoking domain unless exceptions related to specific internal targets apply. In the current example, with the output parameter priceDeliveryInformation a target relaxation is contained in the EWSRS indicating that values returned in this parameter may be passed to the parameter infoSupplier1 of Web service calculateOffer in domain B. In addition, the EWSRS indicates that values returned by this Web service may be used as input parameters of Web services internal to domain B, an indication with no specific meaning in this case since the only output parameter is visibility-restricted with an exception referring to an input parameter of a specific Web service in domain B. In other cases, this indication would allow output parameters without visibility restriction to be used throughout domain B as input parameters of internal Web services.

5.3   Approach to Reduce Complexity of Security Policy Statements

In cases where the differentiation between allowed and disallowed semantics (mainly relating to allowed and disallowed processing of information within a remotely defined business process) would be too complicated leading to complex rules in the corresponding security policy statement, the complexity may be reduced in a manner described in this section.

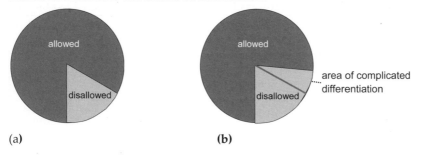

(a)   (b)

Figure 10: Steps for Reduction of Complexity of Security Policy Statement (Part 1)

In Figure 10a, the allowed and disallowed semantics of a remotely defined business process is depicted within the circle. Consider the situation where part of the allowed semantics would impose complicated differentiation from disallowed semantics as indicated in Figure 10b by the differently coloured section in the allowed part. In order to reduce the complexity of the security policy statement, a local Web service could be established providing the semantics represented by this area. This is indicated in Figure 11a by the section taken out of the circle. After having defined a Web service for this purpose, there is no longer any need for a business process to encompass this part of the allowed semantics as part of its intrinsic processing. Instead, a business process can invoke this newly defined Web service for this purpose.

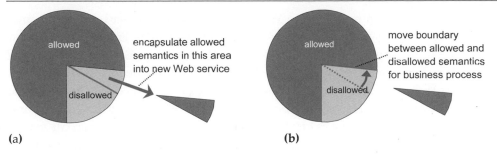

(a)   (b)

Figure 11: Steps for Reduction of Complexity of Security Policy Statement (Part 2)

Since there is no requirement to perform such processing within a business process, this formerly allowed semantics may be forbidden for a business process. Doing so means to move the boundary between allowed and disallowed semantics to enclose the formerly allowed section into the disallowed area. This step is depicted in Figure 11b. In order to disallow the formerly allowed part being used, the security policy statement would drop the complicated specification of the semantics in the removed area.

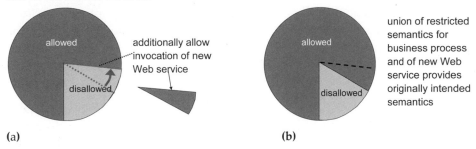

(a)   (b)

Figure 12: Steps for Reduction of Complexity of Security Policy Statement (Part 3)

Further, to allow the new Web service being invoked by a business process, the security policy statement has to be modified as indicated in Figure 12a. The new security policy would instead add the new Web service to the list of local Web services allowed to be invoked.

Finally, the complicated differentiation between allowed and disallowed semantics in the security policy statement can be avoided, still preserving the originally allowed semantics of Figure 10a as the overall semantics for a business process. However, as indicated in Figure 12b, the original semantics now is provided by the union of the semantics of the new Web service and the remaining allowed semantics for the business process.

5.4 Coping with Dynamic Aspects in Static Compliance Analysis

The approach presented in the former sections relies on static analysis of a BPEL script prior to execution. Therefore, this approach inherently is not suited to be applied for checking restrictions with respect to Web service invocations that involve dynamic aspects. Obviously, such checking may only be performed at runtime. An example of a restriction to Web service parameters that require dynamic checking can also be given by reference to the example CBP in Figure 4. Consider a restriction of the input parameter listOfItems of Web service checkStock requiring that only items from a predefined set of items are allowed to be included in this list when this Web service is invoked by the control business process on behalf of the car manufacturer. The reasons for such a restriction could be that the gearbox manufacturer produces gearboxes for different car manufacturers and each car manufacturer is only allowed to make inquiries with respect to the gearboxes (or parts thereof) produced for his own types of cars, but not with respect to gearboxes of competitive car manufacturers. Since the contents of this list passed from the invoker of the business process (*i.e.*, from the car manufacturer in this example) will only be known at runtime, any static analysis will fail to assert the observance of this restriction in a BPEL script received from the car manufacturer.

However, similar to the approach to reducing complexity of the restrictions in an SPS introduced in the former section, a method for coping with dynamic aspects of policy-induced restrictions can be provided. While in Section 5.3, parts of the processing logic of a potential business process requiring too complicate a specification of restrictions has been moved to a separate Web service thereby relieving the requirement to express the complex restrictions in the SPS, here for enabling dynamic validation of restrictions, dynamic checks are moved to Web services defined for this purpose.

In this way, checking of restricted value ranges of input parameters that only can be performed at runtime will be moved from the static analysis prior to execution to dynamic analysis during runtime. In order to still validate that a BPEL script conforms to the security policy during pre-execution assessment, the SPS needs to be amended in order to cope with dynamic aspects of compliance assessment. To this end, the input parameter of the Web service with value range restrictions to be checked during runtime will be specified as an input parameter with source restrictions and the Web service containing the dynamic check of this input parameter against the list of allowed values will be indicated as the only allowed source of values for this parameter.

In the example above, a new Web service checkItemListFromDomainA would have to be defined at the site of the gearbox manufacturer (domain B) that would accept the listOfItems passed from the car manufacturer as its input parameter and return this list as output parameter in case its content conformed to the value range restriction with respect to the car manufacturer (domain A). If the check failed, this new Web service could return an empty list to indicate this situation or raise some particular sort of exception. In addition to provide this new Web service, the SPS of domain B with respect to BPEL scripts received from domain A would have to be modified to require that values for the input parameter listOfItems of Web service checkStock are source-restricted (class 6 restriction) with allowed source to be the output parameter of this new Web service `checkItemListFromDomainA`. In this way, it could be checked prior to execution of a BPEL script received from the car manufacturer that the restrictions with respect to the list content passed to the Web service `checkStock` either would have been obeyed or an empty list will get passed to this Web service (possibly causing a fault in this Web service or, alternatively, an exception already would have been raised before invoking this Web service). With this modified SPS, the compliance assessment can still be performed as usual prior to executing a BPEL script and result in a pass verdict even though the actual list contents passed from the car manufacturer is not known at this time. Of course, after this extension to the SPS has been made, a compliant BPEL script from the car manufacturer actually has to invoke the new Web service prior to invoking the Web service `checkStock` and pass the output parameter from this new Web service to the input parameter listOfItems of `checkStock`. Important but not particular to this new Web service is the requirement that provisions are in place to securely prevent tampering of the processing logic of this Web service, particularly from outside domain B or by activities performed in a business process remotely defined and brought into domain B for execution.

This approach to introduce specific Web services for the purpose of performing dynamic compliance checks of Web service parameters at runtime is, to a certain extent, similar to that proposed by Sirer and Wang[147] where also Web services are amended by specific security policy enforcement code to perform dynamic compliance assessment during execution. In their approach, the security policy first has to be expressed in a special purpose specification language based on first order logic and temporal logic. Once security policies have been specified in this formal manner, instrumentation code is generated automatically to be executed as a preamble in Web service invocation. While this approach relies completely on security policy enforcement at runtime, the approach presented here performs as much enforcement as possible during compliance assessment based on static analysis of BPEL scripts prior to execution and uses instrumentation of the business process only for checking that need to be performed at runtime. In contrast to the approach proposed by Sirer and Wang, the additional Web services used herein for checking value (range) restrictions of input parameters of specific Web services are not generated automatically, but have to be hand-coded to suit the particular purposes. This may be considered a drawback compared to the approach of Sirer and Wang. However, rendering specification of security policy in terms of formal logic unnecessary which is the case in the approach proposed here is deemed to over-compensate this possible drawback of not providing automatic generation of Web services for dynamic security checking.

---

147 Sirer and Wang, 2002

5.5 Summary

In this chapter, the transformation of the results from the analysis of BPEL with respect to its intrinsic security relevance into a method to re-formulate the security policies in terms of allowed and disallowed security-relevant semantic patterns in a BPEL script has been described. The purpose of this is to support the compliance assessment of remotely defined BPEL scripts with security policies in force at the executing site in such a manner that this assessment is facilitated considerably and becomes suited to be performed automatically. To this end, a set of checklist-typed tabular forms have been introduced in this chapter that are intended to accommodate the policy-implied rules to be observed by all BPEL scripts coming from a particular remote site. The collection of rules derived from security policies and determined to be relevant in the business process layer is referred to as security policy statement (SPS). The rules indicated in these forms relate to Web services allowed to be invoked by such BPEL scripts. If invocation of a Web service is only acceptable with certain restrictions to its input and output parameters, such restrictions are indicated in special forms on a per Web service basis. Though presented in this chapter in a form intended for human readability, it is obvious that the contents of SPSs have to be converted to a form better suited for machine processing if the compliance assessment is to be performed in an automatic manner. This will be discussed further in Chapter 7.

Though compliance assessment is based on static analysis of a BPEL script prior to its execution that by nature is not able to cope with restrictions only checkable at runtime, an approach to also cover such restrictions as far as possible during static analysis has also been shown. Comparable approaches to the one proposed herein to complement the static compliance assessment towards dynamic aspects of information flow control also have been proposed in related work[148]. Though not original to our research, however, this approach to cope with restrictions that can only be checked dynamically combined with the original work presented here seems to be useful to broaden the applicability of the methods proposed for compliance assessment in practice.

In the next chapter, the process of assessing the compliance of BPEL scripts with security policies will be discussed in more detail. Also, different ways to delegate the task of compliance assessment to dedicated nodes within or outside the security domain of an organisation and to share the resources used for compliance assessment (even across organisational boundaries) will be proposed.

---

148 Sirer and Wang, 2002; Vachharajani *et al.*, 2004

6 Security Policy Compliance Assessment for BPEL Scripts

After analysis of security-relevant behaviour of BPEL and re-specification of security policies in terms of so-called security-relevant semantic patterns of BPEL, the procedure of assessing compliance of remotely defined BPEL scripts with security policies of the executing domain will be described in this chapter. Further, the workflow of cross-organisational deployment of BPEL scripts including assessment of compliance prior to executing them is considered in more detail. Finally, approaches to delegation of compliance assessment in a distributed environment are presented. Hence, this chapter may be of particular interest to readers who want to see how the methods and procedures presented so far can be applied in practice.

6.1 Procedure of Compliance Assessment

The function of compliance assessment as used in the context of the approach presented here is to make sure that only BPEL scripts completely observing the restrictions implied by the security policies of the executing domain will be accepted for execution. Such assessment of a remotely defined BPEL script can be (and usually will be) conducted prior to executing the business process specified by this script. Therefore, the methods proposed here are chosen such that they do not require the business process defined by a particular BPEL script to be executed for testing or monitoring purposes in order to assess its compliance with the policy-induced rules derived from security policies for the business process layer. Since possible violations of such rules can be detected in this way before these violations would be committed by the business process being executed, the approach proposed here provides a very effective way of security policy enforcement. This procedure of assessing compliance with security policies prior to execution may be considered a check point in the sense of security patterns[149].

6.1.1 Prerequisites for Compliance Assessment

The main prerequisite for the compliance assessment besides the BPEL script under consideration is the SPS specified by the executing domain with respect to the remote domain sending a BPEL script for execution and the application context of the business process to be defined by this script. Furthermore, the WSDL definitions of all Web services indicated in the SPS are required. Finally, the WSDL

---

149 Yoder and Barcalow, 1997

definition of the Web service provided by the business process resulting from execution of the BPEL script will be required, in particular in cases where this WSDL definition is specified beforehand by the executing domain in order to indicate the required Web service this business process has to provide to its environment. In the latter case, the messages to be exchanged with the environment are predefined and, therefore, are likely to be addressed in the SPS if subject to security policy-implied restrictions. If, for example, the predefined input messages to be accepted by the business process under consideration are restricted with respect to particular value ranges (class 4 restrictions), then this could be indicated in the SPS as a restriction to the internal Web service that is going to be provided by this business process[150]. Since the names of the Web service and its input and output parameters will be known from the WSDL definition, restrictions with respect to its input and output parameters can be specified in the SPS.

If such a WSDL definition of the Web service provided by the business process under consideration is not available beforehand because, for example, this definition is provided by the site specifying the BPEL script and varies between different BPEL scripts coming from this site, then this WSDL definition usually will not be available at the time when an SPS is specified and, thus, restrictions to input and output parameters of this Web service cannot be included in the SPS. Nevertheless, restrictions to input and output parameters of this Web service may be implied by other restrictions in the SPS. For instance, one restriction generally applicable to messages sent to an invoker of the Web service in a reply to a message received from this invoker states that such outgoing messages must never contain any visibility-restricted information unless the receiver of this message is indicated as an allowed external target of this information. Even though not addressed in the SPS, the WSDL definition of the business process under consideration is usually required for the purpose of information flow analysis to be conducted during compliance assessment.

6.1.2   Analysis of Declaration Part in BPEL Script

Given all these prerequisites are available, the process of compliance assessment can start with searching the partner link declarations of the BPEL script for Web services invoked by the business process. Each Web service found this way has to be present in the SPS since this contains an exhaustive list of all Web services allowed to be invoked with or without further restrictions. A Web service found in a partner link declaration, but not in the SPS, could still be acceptable if it can be verified by static analysis of the BPEL script that the particular partner link will not be used in the process definition part. If this cannot be verified or if a more rigo-

---

150   Though this Web service will usually be invoked from outside the executing domain, it
      is considered an internal Web service of the executing domain because it will be
      provided within this domain.

rous approach is taken not to accept any Web service in the declaration part that is not indicated in the SPS (independent of its actual use in the business process), then the assessment of the BPEL script already is terminated here with a fail verdict that means the BPEL script does not comply with the applicable security policy.

6.1.3 Checking BPEL Script for Security-Relevant Semantic Patterns

If the BPEL script has passed this first stage of compliance assessment, then the parts defining the process logic have to be searched for invocations of Web services allowed by the SPS. For every Web service invocation it is checked whether for the particular Web service there are restrictions associated with its input and output parameters in the SPS. If restrictions are found, their obedience has to be assessed. For restrictions of classes 3, 5, and 6, information flow analysis in forward or backward direction has to be performed as required. Restrictions of class 4 may be checked by simply verifying that optional input parameters are provided if they are indicated as required or not used if indicated as forbidden. During information flow analysis in forward direction with respect to visibility-restricted information, care has to be taken to watch out for possible covert channels of information flow. Semantic patterns susceptible for the establishment of covert channels have already been identified in Tables 2 and 3 above. Therefore, it is known what to look for with respect to covert channel detection during compliance assessment.

6.1.4 Example of Covert Channel Establishment in BPEL Script

An example for the establishment of a covert channel is depicted in Figure 13. Suppose that Web service WS_A has an output parameter priceA indicating the price of an item A that is visibility-restricted (class 3 restriction), that is, it must not be leaked to an information sink outside the executing domain. This Web service is invoked and its output parameter priceA is assigned to a variable P. After this assignment, a branch occurs in the process flow using an if activity. The branching condition depends on the variable P containing the visibility-restricted price of item A. If this value is smaller than 100 currency units (of an arbitrary currency that does not matter in this example), then the process flow branches to the invocation of a Web service WS_1. If the value is greater than or equal 100 currency units, then Web service WS_2 is invoked.

If at least one or even both of these Web services WS_1 and WS_2 are external Web services (*e.g.*, Web services within the domain where the BPEL script was specified) or happen to exhibit otherwise externally observable behaviour, then by observing the behaviour of the business process defined by the BPEL script containing the snippet in Figure 13 conclusions can be drawn on the price of item A. Supposing that only the invocation of Web service WS_1 is observable from outside the executing domain then, if the observer recognises that W_1 is invoked (either directly because WS_1 resides in the domain of the observer or indirectly via the externally observable behaviour of WS₁), he knows that this price is below 100 currency units. Otherwise, if the invocation of WS₁ cannot be observed, the observer who can be assumed to know the BPEL script because it was specified at his site can conclude from this observation that WS₁ has not been invoked at that point in the business process but that WS₂ has been invoked and, therefore, that the price of item A is greater than or equal to 100 currency units. Thus, a covert channel relating to the visibility-restricted information on the price of item A would have been established by the snippet of a BPEL script in Figure 13.

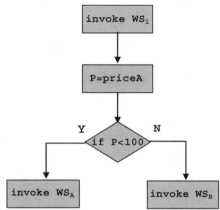

Figure 13: Covert Channel Example

It can easily be seen that the leakage of information relating to the price of item A that is only at a very coarse level in this example (either P<100 or P≥100) can be refined to arbitrary granularity by cascading a series of such branching dependent on the value of variable P. In order to avoid such covert channels, any flow control decision based on class 3 restricted information would be banned here and, therefore, when detected in compliance assessment, would cause a BPEL script containing such semantic patterns to be considered non-conformant to the security policies under consideration. Note that this rigorous approach to cope with avoidance of covert channels could be relaxed by applying more sophisticated algorithms for covert channels detection, for instance, checking whether alternative flows selected by branching on visibility-restricted information actually exhibits any distinguishing behaviour observable from outside. However, elaborating such algorithms is beyond the scope of the approaches presented here and, therefore, left for further studies. To get an impression how such algorithms could look like, the reader is referred to Appendix 2 containing an outline of more sophisticated covert channel prevention in conjunction with activity `validate`.

6.1.5   Information Flow Analysis in Parallel Flows

Besides covert channel detection, also analysis of information flow in parallel flows needs further consideration. During this analysis, actual and potential parallel flows are distinguished. Actual parallel flows are those specified in parallel versions of forEach activities or in flow activities without any links that restrict the activities contained in a flow activity from being performed in parallel. These parallel flows will actually be performed in parallel when the business process is executed. By contrast, potential parallel flows will not be performed in parallel during business process execution but only specify alternatives for the flow of business logic from which only one at a time will actually be chosen during execution. Such potential parallel flows are presented by the alternate flows in an if activity and in a pick activity as well as the flows specified in event handlers, fault handlers (including flows specified in compensation handlers initiated by those fault handlers), and termination handlers. The flows specified in these handlers can be considered alternate flows to the main flow of the process since the reason for activating the flows specified in these handlers may occur at any time during normal process execution. For example, the activities in a fault handler will be executed instead of the main process flow when the corresponding exception caught by this fault handler occurs. This usually can happen at virtually every moment during process execution. Therefore, fault handlers establish potential parallel flows to each other and to the part of the process (a particular scope or the whole process) to which they relate. The same is true for event handlers and termination handlers.

For the purpose of information flow analysis, actual and potential flows are not distinguished since the static analysis performed here considers all potential flows in a process at once instead of only one actual choice of them as will be the case during business process execution. For instance, when analysing information flow in backward direction as required for restrictions of classes 5 and 6 applicable to input parameters of a Web service invoked, all potential values that could have been assigned to a variable that will be passed as a particular restricted input parameter have to be considered. Hence, all parallel flows in backward direction from the Web service invocation towards the start of the business process have to be checked for assignments to the particular variable irrespective of whether these flows are actual parallel flows or only potential parallel flows. If at least one value assigned to this variable in any of the (actual or potential) parallel flows would contradict the restriction imposed to the input parameter of the Web service for which the variable is used as actual value, then a violation of the SPS would have been detected resulting in a fail verdict for the compliance assessment. Although the process described may appear to be complicated, an implementation of this process (or at least important parts of it) in a prototype has shown that the proposed approach to compliance assessment of BPEL scripts prior to execution is viable and appropriate for automatic processing. Of course, the notation of an SPS as introduced here in a tabular form that accommodates human readability will have to be converted into another form that is better suited for machine processing. This will be explained in further detail in Chapter 7.

6.2 Workflows in Distributed Definition and Execution of CBPs

In this section, a set of workflows will be defined that combine the tasks required in defining, deploying, assessing and executing BPEL-defined business processes in such a manner that the temporal order of them is clarified. If CBPs are defined and executed in a distributed manner as discussed in earlier chapters, the definition, deployment, and assessment of compliance with security policies prior to execution represent a workflow of its own that is not considered part of executing the business process being defined by a cross-organisational deployed BPEL script. In fact, even several separate sub-workflows can be distinguished in the approach to security policy enforcement proposed in this project. On the executing side, when the approaches proposed here are to be used, prior to acceptance of any remotely defined BPEL script from a foreign domain, an SPS has to be assembled to define the security policies in a way that is well-suited for compliance assessment of the BPEL scripts accepted for execution. The tasks involved here are depicted in the workflow diagram of Figure 14. As in the example of a CBP in Figure 4, the executing domain is denoted domain B and the domain defining BPEL scripts for execution in domain B is denoted domain A. The workflow of Figure 14 will be performed within domain B. In general, domain B can allow different domains to bring in BPEL scripts for execution. To differentiate between these different domains, an index is added to the domain identifier (*e.g.*, domain A_i)

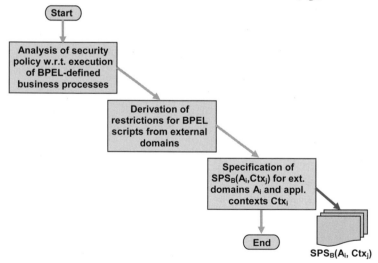

Figure 14: Workflow for Specification of Security Policy Statements

The workflow in Figure 14 starts with an analysis of local security policies to determine which parts of them are relevant at the business process layer. As already discussed in Chapter 4, for example, providing secure communication between partners in a distributed environment is treated at layers below the business process layer. After determination of the security policy-implied rules that are relevant at the business process layer, the restrictions for cross-domain deployed BPEL scripts for the different domains A_i potentially sending such scripts to the executing domain B are derived from these rules.

As a final step in this workflow, the security policy statements are specified for all foreign domains A_i that will be allowed to send BPEL scripts for execution and for all application contexts Ctx_j that are to be distinguished when assessing such scripts for compliance with local security policies. The SPS for the i-th foreign domain and the j-th application context is denoted $SPS_B(A_i, Ctx_j)$ where the index B is there to indicate that this is an SPS representing the security policy of domain B.

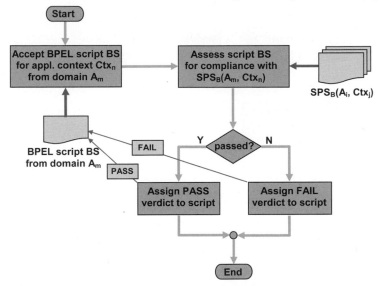

Figure 15: Workflow for Compliance Assessment of BPEL Script

Defining a BPEL script in domain A_i and sending it to domain B for execution constitutes a second workflow not depicted in a figure herein because of its trivial nature. This workflow in domain A_i corresponds to the workflow in domain B shown in Figure 15. In this workflow, domain B receives a BPEL script BS for a particular application context Ctx_n from a domain A_m. In the next step, the appropriate security policy statement $SPS_B(A_m, Ctx_n)$ is retrieved and used for compliance assessment of script BS with the local security policies in domain B. As discussed in Chapter 5, given all restrictions derived from security policies relevant at the business process layer have been formulated in terms of allowed and disallowed semantic patterns of BPEL, the security assessment can be performed prior to execution as a straightforward look-up of the script for allowed patterns and the validation that no disallowed information flow (explicit or implicit) occurs. If the script BS passes the assessment, then a verdict of PASS is assigned to this script. Otherwise, a verdict of FAIL will be assigned to it. It is taken for granted that appropriate provisions are made in the executing domain B to prevent tampering the BPEL script and the verdict assigned to it before and during its execution. Supplying a modification-secure checksum to the script and its verdict, for example, may be a means to fulfil this requirement.

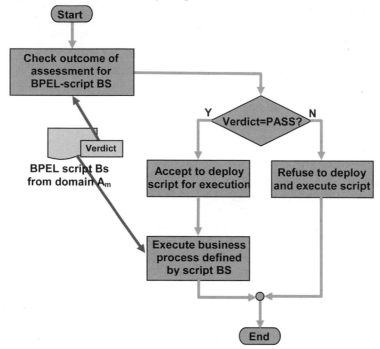

Figure 16: Workflow for Deployment and Execution of BPEL Script

As a final workflow, the deployment and execution of the business process being defined by the BPEL script BS is depicted in Figure 16. This workflow, again, is performed in domain B. Before deployment and execution of script BS, this workflow checks the verdict assigned to the script by the workflow in Figure 15. After termination of this workflow, a BPEL script with a PASS verdict is installed on an appropriate platform of domain B in such a way that it can be used as part of a CBP spanning at least the domains A_m and B. This implies that invocation of the business process (more precisely, invocation of the Web service provided by this business process) will be possible and allowed for invokers from domain A_m (*i.e.*, the defining domain of the script BS).

6.3   Delegation of Security Policy Compliance Assessment

Even with the definition of SPS in the manner described in Chapter 5, the task of analysing security-relevant semantics of BPEL scripts and matching against restrictions imposed by policies still is not, in every case, trivial and it might not always be capable of being performed automatically. Therefore, it may be desirable to reduce the effort for installing appropriate resources in the executing domain by not having the workflow of Figure 15 performed at every node in domain B that will execute remotely defined BPEL scripts. This can be achieved by delegation of at least part of the compliance assessment to dedicated locations. Based on the consideration of the workflows involved as described in the former section, several approaches to distribution of the tasks between different nodes in a cross-organisational environment will be discussed. This distribution may occur within the domain executing the BPEL script under consideration or across domain boundaries.

6.3.1   Domain-Internal Delegation of Compliance Assessment

A promising approach to reducing the effort of compliance assessment is the delegation of parts of the assessment to a dedicated node within a domain B instead of performing this task at every node in this domain. That means that the steps of compliance assessment (step 2) and assigning the verdict related to the outcome of this assessment to the script under consideration (step 3) in the workflow depicted in Figure 15 may be delegated to a dedicated node in domain B. This node is called security assessment centre (SAC) for domain B. Hence, this node is labelled B$_{SAC}$. Advantages related to this delegation of security assessment to a domain-internal SAC include that human interaction, if required during the assessment of scripts with respect to compliance with security restrictions, may be more easily provided at a single node (or only few nodes, if single point of failure would be an issue) in a domain compared to the situation of being distributed across the domain. It may also facilitate use of specific software required for this purpose since it only needs to be available at a single instance both with respect to potential license fees and effort for user training.

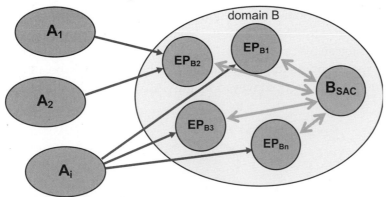

Figure 17: Domain-Internal Delegation of Security Assessment

In Figure 17, this domain-internal delegation is illustrated. After delegation to node B$_{SAC}$, all other nodes in domain B would access this specific node before executing a remotely defined BPEL script. This security look-up requires, that the BPEL script in question be sent to node B$_{SAC}$ by any executing node (node EP$_{B1}$, EP$_{B2}$, EP$_{B3}$, ..., EP$_{Bn}$, in the example of Figure 17 where EP means executing platform) together with an indication of the domain from where the BPEL script originates, say A$_m$, and the application context for which the script is intended for, say Ctx$_k$. On completion, the results of the assessment process will be sent back from node B$_{SAC}$ to the node sending the inquiry for assessment, say node EP$_{Bn}$, and depending on the result, the BPEL script may be executed on node EP$_{Bn}$ or not. Since the SPS$_B$(A$_m$, Ctx$_k$) of domain B with respect to domain A$_m$ as the origin of the BPEL script and the application context Ctx$_k$ may be supposed to be already available at node B$_{SAC}$, there is no requirement to also transmit this SPS from node EP$_{Bn}$ to node B$_{SAC}$ in conjunction with the BPEL script.

6.3.2   Domain-External Delegation of Compliance Assessment

In cases where several domains in a CBP context allow for mutual exchange of BPEL scripts and their execution (provided they comply to the respective local security policies), the analysis and assessment could further be centralised to a particular node shared by all domains for this purpose. This node would desirably be a node external to all domains involved in the particular CBP context in order to avoid conflict of interest as much as possible. Such a domain-independent assessment centre (denoted E$_{SAC}$) is shown in Figure 18. After delegation has taken place, nodes of all domains accepting BPEL scripts from other domains in this CBP context would inquire node E$_{SAC}$ for security assessment when they receive a new script for execution.

In this case, not only the BPEL script subject to security assessment and the indication of its origin and application context has to be conveyed to the assessment centre, but also the SPS against which compliance assessment is required has to be provided to the SAC. This could be done prior to sending the BPEL script for assessment, for instance, at the time when a domain subscribes to the assessment service by sending all relevant SPSs to the SAC. Sending SPSs to the SAC would also be required each time an SPS changes or a new SPS has been defined. Alternatively, the SPS for a specific originating domain can also be sent each time a BPEL script received from this domain is conveyed to the SAC for compliance assessment.

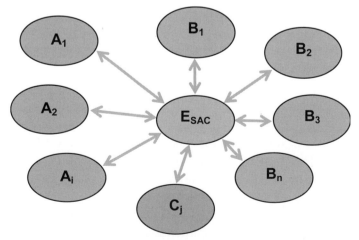

Figure 18: Outsourcing of Security Assessment

While security and trust aspects do not necessarily play a central role if the delegation of the assessment task takes place within one single domain, these aspects become important if delegation occurs across domain boundaries. Further, if the assessment task is outsourced to a node outside the own domain, say E$_{SAC}$ as shown in Figure 18, the communication to and from node E$_{SAC}$ is required to be secure both with respect to authentication and data integrity. The results of assessing a particular BPEL script must unambiguously be attributed as coming from the SAC and have not been forged on their way back to the node mandating the assessment. Since mechanisms for achieving authenticated communication and providing integrity of information conveyed over a communication channel are well-known, appropriate provisions are taken for granted and, therefore, this aspect is not discussed in further detail.

However, the issue of privacy of information contained in security policies that have to be conveyed to the external assessment service, as well as the issue of trust implied in this delegation of assessment, have to be considered in order to render this approach feasible (*e.g.*, questions with respect to trustworthiness of the results returned by the assessment centre have to be coped with). Furthermore, if assessment is delegated to a third party serving several domains, possible conflict of interest may become an issue if the SAC serves both the originating domain and the executing domain of a BPEL script. These aspects need to be considered carefully before taking the approach to install a centralised assessment centre for domain-independent use by different partners involved in a CBP context. However, detailed considerations concerning trust relations required in such a delegation process were beyond the scope of consideration in this book.

6.4 Summary

In this chapter, based on the re-specification of the security policies of the executing site leading to a so-called SPS as introduced in Chapter 5, it has been described how the compliance assessment of a BPEL script under consideration actually can be conducted as a check for observance of the restrictions indicated in the SPS in a manner similar to a desk check that is without any requirement to execute the script for checking purposes. Most of the restrictions to be followed relate to information flow. Thus, the information flow in a BPEL script has to be analysed in order to check the compliance to these restrictions. As a special aspect, information flow analysis in potential parallel flows (*i.e.*, alternate flows in a business process to be chosen at runtime) has to be conducted. It turned out that for the purpose of static information flow prior to execution, potential parallel flows have to be treated quite the same as actual parallel flows in a business process. As already pointed out in the former chapter, detection of potential covert channels that may be suited to leak protected information in an indirect manner by selection between different embodiments of observable behaviour of a business process dependent on such information is also very important.

The different workflows involved in deployment of BPEL-defined business processes across organisational boundaries and in compliance assessment with security policies of the executing domain have also been discussed in this chapter. Ways of delegating the task of compliance assessment from the particular node where a BPEL script is executed to a centralised assessment centre within the same domain as the executing node or to a domain-external assessment centre serving several domains has been discussed. In particular, with delegation of compliance assessment beyond the boundaries of one's own domain, the issues with respect to privacy of information contained in security policies and to trust with respect to the results returned if domain-external assessment is employed have been addressed. However, the latter aspects were beyond the scope of considerations in this book.

Having developed in the former chapters the approaches to facilitate security policy compliance assessment of remotely defined business processes based on a thorough analysis of security-relevant semantics of BPEL and making use of a specified form of security policy definition (called SPS in this project), the proof of concept for these approaches provided by developing a prototype to show their viability and suitability for automatic processing will be described in the next chapter.

7 Proof of Concept by Prototypical Implementation

In the former chapters, the ideas constituting the approach presented here have been developed and described in detail. In particular, the definition of SPS to facilitate the process of compliance assessment was explained and the procedure of checking a BPEL script for its compliance with local security policies has been outlined. In order to provide an effective and efficient method for security policy enforcement in the context of business process execution, particularly in scenarios where the corresponding BPEL scripts defining the processes have been defined remotely from the location of their execution, the procedure of compliance assessment should preferably be capable of being performed automatically (at least major parts thereof).

Although the aim from the outset was to potentially come up with methods that are suited for automatic processing, it is not clear from their description in the former chapters that this goal has actually been reached. Therefore, a prototype has been developed that implements essential aspects of the ideas proposed. The purpose of this prototype was to serve as proof of concept for the viability of the approach. The prototypical implementation is presented in this chapter and it is discussed to what extent the proof of concept has been achieved in this way.

Hence, readers who want to get a deeper look at structures and algorithms that may be useful in automatic performance of the approach to compliance assessment introduced in the former chapters may be particularly interested to read this chapter while others not specifically interested in programming details may skip this chapter.

7.1 Scope of Prototypical Implementation

Before starting the development of the prototype, the scope of the proof of concept and the resulting requirements with respect to the functionality to be covered by the prototype were established.

As already mentioned in Chapter 4, the BPEL standard has undergone modifications during the course of the research that provided the current approaches to compliance assessment of business processes with security policies. While the results presented in Chapters 4 and 5 have been adapted to the version of BPEL that finally has been adopted as an OASIS standard[151], the work on the prototype started before this version was available and, hence, has been based on a former ver-

---

151 Alves *et al.*, 2007

sion of BPEL[152] that distinguishes from the latest version with respect to some activities added or renamed during the last phases of the standardisation process. However, the principles of automatic compliance assessment based on an SPS can also be demonstrated using the former names of the activities in question.

Since the essential purpose of the prototype is to demonstrate that the approach developed and presented in the former chapters is actually suited for automatic processing, the implementation is restricted to a representative subset of the potential functionality. However, the selected elements had to cover all aspects that were essential and predominantly new in this approach. As a starting point for selecting the functionality to be incorporated, the indications in Tables 2 and 3 with respect to the security relevance of the different semantic patterns were taken. These indications denote the required checking to be performed during compliance assessment in order to verify whether the particular restriction is obeyed or not. The coverage of the different checkings occurring in these tables that are provided by the prototype is indicated in Table 4.

Table 4: Coverage of Checking Functionality by Prototype

Checking Type	Purpose of Check	Coverage
IFA(v)	Check visibility restriction by information flow analysis in forward direction	I
IFA(r)	Check value range restriction by information flow analysis in backward direction (see note 1)	T/N
IFA(s)	Check source restriction by information flow analysis in backward direction	I
u	Check whether usage of optional input parameter complies to restriction of options (forbidden or required)	T
time(v)	Check that no visibility-restricted information is used to determine timeout period	D
except(v)	Check that no visibility-restricted information is used to determine exception to be thrown or be included as part of exception data passed along with the exception	D
exit(v)	Check that no visibility-restricted information is used to determine reason for termination	D
scope(v)	Check that no visibility-restricted information is used to determine `<scope>` to be compensated (see note 2)	D
val(v)	Check that visibility-restricted information are not type-validated with respect to types implying restricted ranges of allowed values (see note 3)	D/E

152   Arkin *et al.*, 2004

Checking Type	Purpose of Check	Coverage
branch cond(v)	Check that no visibility-restricted information is used to determine branch to be selected in alternate flows (see note 4)	I
loop cond(v)	Check that no visibility-restricted information is used to determine conditions controlling the iteration in a `while` or `repeatUntil` activity	D
iteration bound(v)	Check that no visibility-restricted information is used to determine bounds of iteration in a consecutive or parallel version of `forEach` activity (see note 5)	D
preempt(v)	Check that no visibility-restricted information is used to determine condition for pre-emptive termination of a `forEach` activity (see note 5)	D

I   Type of checking implemented

D   Type of checking not implemented, but implementation easily deducible from covert channel detection scheme as implemented for the **switch** activity

T   Type of checking not implemented, but implementation considered trivial

N   Type of checking not suitable for static analysis since requiring dynamic checking at runtime (viable by the scheme outlined in Section 5.4).

E   Type of checking not implemented requiring non-trivial extension of current functionality (see note 3)

Note 1: Checking of value range restrictions during static analysis is either trivial (if constant values specified within the BPEL script are involved) or impossible during static analysis (if dynamic values extracted from messages received during runtime are involved)

Note 2: The **compensateScope** activity requiring this type of checking has been introduced comparatively late during the standardisation process of BPEL. However, similar to checking for covert channel detection with other activities, its implementation is deducible in an easy way from the covert channel detection scheme implemented for the **switch** activity.

Note 3: The **validate** activity has been introduced very late during the standardisation process of BPEL. Therefore, checking for covert channels with this activity is not implemented. As long as it is acceptable to prevent type validation of variables containing visibility-restricted information, this check can be implemented as a straightforward extension of the covert channel detection scheme implemented for the **switch** activity. In this case, the indication D applies. However, if this approach is considered to be overly strict, then a more sophisticated algorithm has to be implemented as outlined in Appendix 2 that cannot be considered easily deducible from the covert channel detection scheme implemented for the **switch** activity. In this case, the indication E applies.

Note 4: At the time the prototype was conceived, the branching functionality in BPEL was expressed by the **switch** activity that has been covered by the prototype implementation. Lately during the standardisation process of BPEL, the **switch** activity has been replaced by the **if** activity providing the same functionality.

Note 5 The **forEach** activity has been introduced lately during the standardisation process of BPEL. The two new types of checking for covert channel detection required
with this new activity (check that neither the iteration bounds nor the conditions
for possible pre-emptive termination of the activity depend on visibility-restricted
information) are deducible in an easy way from the covert channel detection
scheme implemented for the **switch** activity.

As can be seen from the last column in Table 4, aside from two exceptions, all types
of checking required during the compliance assessment process described in the
previous chapters have either been implemented in the prototype (I) or can be
implemented in a trivial manner (T) or its implementation can be deduced from
other implemented checking in a straightforward manner (D).

The two exceptions are the checks for observation of value range restrictions in the
case of dynamic values (*i.e.*, values only know at runtime because they result from
inbound messages received by the business process) being passed in a outgoing
message (marked N in Table 4), and the checks for covert channel prevention with
the validate activity (marked E in Table 4). In the first instance, this type of
checking cannot be performed during static analysis of a BPEL script prior to
execution since it requires dynamic checking only possible at runtime. However,
an approach to cover the requirements for dynamic checking during static analysis
as far as possible has been described already in Section 5.4. Following this approach, dynamic checking for compliance to value range restrictions (class 5 restrictions, denoted by IFA(r) in Table 2) is converted to source restrictions (class 6
restrictions, denoted by IFA(s) in Table 2). Since the checking for compliance to
source restrictions is implemented in the prototype, this type of checking may be
considered covered by the prototype as far as possible by its nature.

With respect to information flow analysis, the prototype was required to cover
(real or potential) parallel flows in a BPEL script under consideration. That means,
if a value is passed in an outbound message (either in an invoke activity or in a
reply activity), then it has to be checked that no visibility-restricted information
encountered in any parallel flows possibly being extracted from an inbound message (either in an invoke activity, a receive activity, or a pick activity) occurred
before this point in a BPEL script will be included in this message.

The prototype has been designed in such a way that it analyses the main activity in
the <process> element of a BPEL script which is typically a sequence activity. The
support of <scope> elements contained in a process definition was not deemed to
be required for the prototype since these elements simply serve structuring
purposes to limit the scope of declarations and to provide a nested structure as
known from other programming languages. This nesting of scopes does not
contribute to the security relevance of the behaviour specified in a BPEL script.
However, it slightly complicates information flow analysis, as scopes of variable
definitions would have to be observed. For instance, if variable A would contain
visibility-restricted information I_1 from a Web service invocation and would be

declared again in an inner scope, then assignment of another information I_2 to variable A within this inner scope (assumed to be not visibility-restricted) would only conceal the visibility-restricted information I_1. Thus, passing variable A in an outbound message to an external Web service within this scope would not violate the security policy. However, once the inner scope is left, the variable A would again contain the visibility-restricted information I_1. Therefore, passing variable A in an outbound message to an external Web service in the containing scope would violate the security policy. In principle, keeping track of re-declarations of the same variable in nested scopes does not pose a problem for the implementation of the assessment process but only increases the complexity of the storage management used for the purpose of information flow analysis (see Section 7.4.3 below).

The checking of links in flow activities (cf. Section 4.2.3) was not considered for implementation in the prototype. Such links are security-relevant if the flow control effectuated by these constructs is made dependent on visibility-restricted information. Checks that are required to prevent the establishment of covert channels using links are very similar to the check branch cond(v) that are required for covert channel prevention with if activities. Since this checking has been implemented in the prototype (in conjunction with the former switch activity), the similar checks for links were not deemed to contribute new insights if implemented in the prototype. Ignoring links that are not dependent on visibility-restricted information may possibly make the assessment process overly strict, as sequential flow potentially induced by such links would be neglected in backward information flow analysis. However, this can only lead to refusal of BPEL scripts as non-compliant that could be accepted as compliant if the sequential flow caused by such links would have been honoured during information flow analysis. It is important that ignoring links not involving visibility-restricted information for flow control purposes can by no means lead to false acceptance of BPEL scripts that actually are not compliant with security policies. These considerations justified the decision to disregard links in the prototype.

As for the different handlers a BPEL script may contain (event handler, termination handler, fault handler, compensation handler), these are also not supported by the prototype since this also would only increase the complexity of the implementation without contributing new insights. As discussed in Section 4.4.2, all such handlers except event handlers do not contribute security-relevant semantics but only increase complexity of information flow analysis since all these handlers represent potential parallel flows in addition to the main activity in a BPEL script. However, treatment of parallel flows in information flow analysis already has been catered for in the prototype such that supporting these handlers would not introduce new aspects to the implementation.

Event handlers that contribute security-relevant behaviour to a business process may be treated in a similar manner as the pick activity as also argued above in

Section 4.4.2. As can be seen from Table 3, the `pick` activity requires both the IFA(v) type of checking and the time(v) type of checking. Table 4 shows that these both types of checking are covered by the prototype (implemented or deducible from implemented functionality). Therefore, support of event handlers in the prototype has been deemed non-essential for the proof of concept and, hence, is not provided.

The essential question to be answered by the proof of concept was to demonstrate that checking for compliance between a BPEL script and restrictions indicated in an SPS could be performed automatically with as little as possible human intervention. Therefore, it was regarded as sufficient to implement the prototype as a stand-alone program not intended to be integrated in a BPEL-enabled platform. Being able to perform the compliance assessment of a BPEL script with the aid of a separate program, which can be executed on any machine with an appropriate Java runtime environment, makes it possible to keep a BPEL script isolated from the BPEL-enabled platform where it is supposed to be executed once it has been assessed successfully. This may even be considered an additional security benefit because even loading a BPEL script into the machine that runs the BPEL-enabled platform just to assess its compliance to security policies can be avoided. Thereby, yet the theoretical risk is securely eliminated that a script could be harmful even prior to its execution by simply loading it into the machine capable of executing BPEL scripts.

7.2 Machine-Readable Format of Security Policy Statement

While the examples of SPS and its components in Chapter 5 were given in human-readable tabular format, it is obvious that it is straightforward to define appropriate XML schemas in order to be capable of presenting the information in machine-processible form. Details of this XML-based format will be explained in this section. In particular, it is argued why existing approaches to expressing access control policies in terms of Path[153], or standardised formalisms for expressing security policies as provided in XACML[154], or SAML[155] have not been adopted and extended for being used for the proposed approach to express restrictions on allowed semantics of BPEL.

A complete XML-based formal specification for the SPS used in the approach to security policy assessment is contained in Appendix 1. While the schema is provided there using the formalisms of XML Schema[156], the excerpts shown in this chapter use a more condensed notation oriented on the meta syntax of regular ex-

---

153 Fundulaki and Marx, 2004; Kuper *et al.*, 2005
154 Moses, 2005
155 Cantor *et al.*, 2005
156 Thompson *et al.*, 2004

pressions. This compact form of schema representation is also used in the BPEL specification[157]. The notational conventions are explained there[158] and provide the following meta characters for indicating repetition of elements and optional parts. An asterisk sign (*) behind an XML element indicates that zero, one or more occurrences of that element being allowed at this place. Similarly, a plus sign (+) behind an XML element means that one or more occurrences are allowed. In addition, a question mark (?) behind an XML element identifies an optional element that may occur once or may be absent. Finally, alternate choices are denoted by a bar (|) between alternatives.

7.2.1 Rationale for Definition of XML Schema in Current Form

The XML schema for the SPS was specified without any recourse to existing approaches for specifying security policies either from standardisation such as SAML[159] or XACML[160] or from research[161]. Reason for this was that none of these approaches comprises means of expressing the aspects of security policies that were relevant in this context. On the other hand, defining the required XML schema based on an existing approach to specify security policies would have implied too much an overhead that would have been inherited this way. It has been decided that definition of the required XML schema for SPS based on such approaches only would have unnecessarily complicated the implementation of the prototype without offering any significant advantages. In contrast, specifying an XML schema to the very purposes of the proof of concept envisaged could result in a much more streamlined definition and, therefore, any overhead imposing additional effort to the implementation of the prototype could be avoided. The proof of concept achievable with the prototype was not diminished by not using an XML schema based on any existing approach for expressing security semantics.

7.2.2 Annotated SPS Schema in Condensed Notation

In order to explain the XML schema that has been provided to specify an SPS in a machine-readable form, the notational conventions as described above are used to depict parts of the schema in a condensed way. In Appendix 1, the overall structure of an SPS is shown.

The element `<identifications>` indicates the domain defining the BPEL script and the domain where it is to be executed in the attributes `remoteDomain` and `localDomain`, respectively. The application context the SPS relates to can be specified in the attribute `applicationContext`. For instance, for the car manufacturer

---

157 Alves *et al.*, 2007
158 *ibid.*, p. 9
159 Cantor *et al.*, 2005
160 Moses, 2005
161 *e.g.*, Sirer and Wang, 2002

from the example in Figure 4, a different set of security policy derived restrictions could apply if he would also be entitled to remotely define business processes in the context of communicating construction plans for new gearboxes with the gearbox manufacturer.

Listing 3: Overall XML Structure of SPS

```
<sps>
<identifications
remoteDomain="foreignDomain"
localDomain="localDomain"
applicationContext="context"/>
<iwsrs> ... </iwsrs>*
<ewsrs> ... </ewsrs>*
<unrestrIntWs> ... </unrestrIntWs>*
<unrestrExtWs> ... </unrestrExtWs>*
</sps>
```

The elements `<iwsrs>` and `<ewsrs>` denote restrictions with respect to internal and external Web services, respectively, one element for each Web service indicated. Similarly, the elements `<unrestrIntWs>` and `<unrestrExtWs>` denote unrestricted internal and external Web services (class 1), respectively.

In Listing 4, the structure of the element `<iwsrs>` is depicted. The element `<ewsrs>` has a similar internal structure. The element `<operation>` denotes the name of a Web service operation and indicates the corresponding port type by a URI. The `<input>` and `<output>` elements indicate restrictions to the corresponding type of Web service parameters, one for each type of message a Web service operation is able to receive or send, respectively.

Listing 4: Structure of Internal Web Service Restriction Statement

```
<iwsrs>
   <operation    name="operationName"
                 portType="URIofPortType">
      <input>    ... </input>*
      <output>   ... </output>*
   </operation>*
</iwsrs>
```

From Listing 5, the structure of the element `<input>` can be seen. It is used to indicate restrictions applying to the input parameters of a Web service. The element may contain the attribute `sourceRestricted` to indicate whether all input parameters are source restricted (class 6) or not. If this attribute is missing, it defaults to the value false. If so, the required originating Web service(s) for a value to be allowed is indicated in one or more `<service>` element(s) contained in the `<sourceRestriction>` element. More than one such originating Web service may be indicated to allow for alternative sources.

Listing 5: Structure of Restriction Indication for Input Parameters

```
<input message="messageName"
       sourceRestricted="true|false"?>
  <sourceRestriction>
    <service portType=URIofPortType"
            operation="operationName"/>+
  </sourceRestriction>?
  <part name="partName"
        restrictedOptional=
             "presentOrNot|forbiddenPart|requiredPart"?
        sourceRestricted=       "true|false"?
        valueRestricted=        "true|false"?>
    <sourceRestriction>
      <service portType= "URIofPortType"
              operation="operationName"/>+
    </sourceRestriction>?
    <valueRestriction>
      <permittedValue> ... </permittedValue>+
    </valueRestriction>?
  </part>*
</input>
```

In addition, at the part level there is an optional indication (via attribute `restrictedOptional`) whether a specific input parameter in spite of being defined as optional must not be used or is required to be used (class 4). This information is not provided on the message level, that is, for all input parameters at once. Such a shortcut for indicating class 4 restrictions for all input parameters has not been recognised as being required in the schema. It should be noted that having class 4 restrictions for all input parameters is not equivalent to a class 2 restriction for the Web service as a whole.

Listing 6: Structure of Restriction Indication for Output Parameters

```
<output     message="messageName"
            visibilityRestricted="true|false"?>
  <targetRelaxation>
    <domain name="domainURI"/>+
  </targetRelaxation>*
  <part name="partName"
        visibilityRestricted="true|false"?>
    <targetRelaxation>
      <domain name="domainURI"/>+
    </targetRelaxation>*
  </part>*
</output>
```

There may be cases, where it is forbidden to pass any value with a Web service invocation, but still the Web service is allowed to be invoked (without passing any value to it). If not all, but only specific input parameters are restricted, this is indicated in the `<part>` element contained in an `<input>` element. Again, it may be indicated whether an input parameter contained in the message representing the union of all input parameters of a Web service is source restricted or not (class 6). If so, the `<part>` element in turn contains an element `<sourceRestriction>` with the same internal structure as discussed above for the message level.

Furthermore, via the attribute `valueRestricted` it can be indicated at the part level that a specific input parameter may only be used with certain values (class 5). The permitted values are specified in one or more `<permittedValue>` elements contained in the element `<part>`. Obviously, the indication of value restriction is only sensible at the part level, since the permitted values have to be specified separately for each input parameter affected by a class 5 restriction.

To conclude the discussion of the XML schema for SPS, the structure of the element `<output>` is depicted in Listing 6. Similar to the indication of source restriction in the `<input>` element, visibility restriction may be indicated on the message level and on the part level via attribute `visibilityRestricted`. As a special case, visibility restriction may be relaxed to cope with the situation in which one or several domains are allowed to see an otherwise visibility-restricted value.

An example for such a relaxation is the lists of items to be ordered from the sub-suppliers in the example of Figure 4. These lists have their visibility restriction relaxed since they are visibility-restricted to all external domains except the specific sub-supplier the list is intended for.

The relaxation of visibility restriction is indicated by the element `<target-Relaxation>` contained within the `<output>` element and contains one or more `<domain>` elements to indicate the domain(s) to which the output parameter may exceptionally be passed. Similar to the `<input>` element, separate parts of the output message, that is, specific output parameters, could be indicated as being visibility-restricted in one or more elements `<part>` contained in the `<output>` element. If target relaxation applies to specific parts, this is indicated by `<target-Relaxation>` elements contained within the `<part>` elements and specifying the domain(s) to which the parameter may be passed. The structures of `<targetRelaxation>` elements are the same at message level and at part level. It should be noted that in an `<output>` element relating to an internal Web service (*i.e.*, an `<output>` element contained in an `<iwsrs>` element), visibility restriction does not apply to the local security domain where the BPEL script is to be executed. Therefore, in an `<iwsrs>` context, this domain will never be indicated in a `<domain>` element within the element `<targetRelaxation>`.

7.3 Architecture of Prototype

The prototype was implemented using Java because of its known characteristic of platform independence. The prototype was designed to provide a GUI for entering the filenames of the SPS and the BPEL script under consideration as well as to display the outcome of the assessment (cf. Figures 18 and 19). The WSDL definitions of the Web services specified in an SPS to be allowed in a compliant BPEL script as well as of the Web services actually being used in a BPEL script subject to compliance assessment should be made available to the prototype via namespace specifications in the respective header of the XML documents containing the SPS and the BPEL script.

Figure 19 provides an overview of the class hierarchy of the prototype. At the top of the diagram, the class CAnalysator denotes the top-level class of the prototype. This class will be instantiated by the GUI when the "Start" button has been actuated. The classes CSpsWsProducer and CBpelVariableProducer represent the parser and converter to internal representation for the SPS and the declaration part of the BPEL script, respectively.

The classes depicted below the abstract class ASpsWs on the right hand side of the diagram provide the internal representation of the SPS while the classes CBpel-Variable and below on the left hand side are used for the internal representation of variables declared in the BPEL script and the parts possibly contained therein. The abstract class AActivity and the classes derived thereof contain the logic required to perform the compliance assessment checking for the different activities supported by the prototype. As can be seen from the class names, the prototype supports the activities invoke, assign, sequence, flow, and switch.

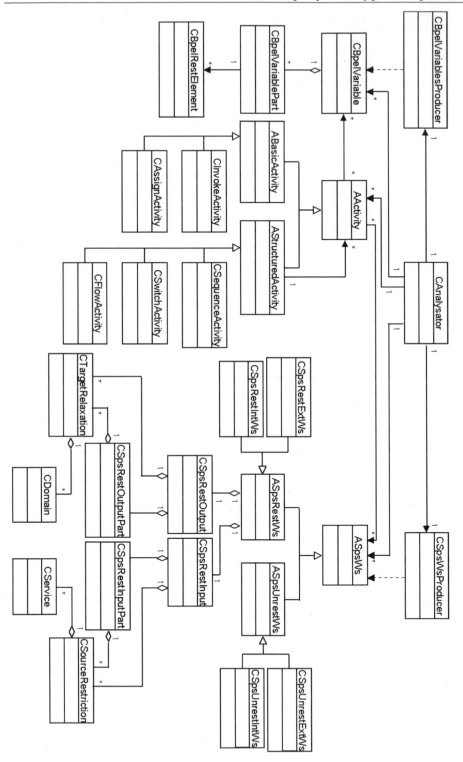

Figure 19: Class Diagram of Prototype

7.4 Functionality of Prototype at a Glance

The BPEL script to be checked and the SPS defining the security policies are input to the prototype. Furthermore, the WSDL definitions[162] of all Web services addressed in the BPEL script under consideration are made available to the prototype. While the names of the files containing the BPEL script and the appropriate SPS have to be entered in the GUI of the prototype, the filenames of the WSDL definitions of the Web services indicated in the SPS as well as of those actually invoked in the BPEL script were provided via namespace declarations in the header of the XML document of the SPS.

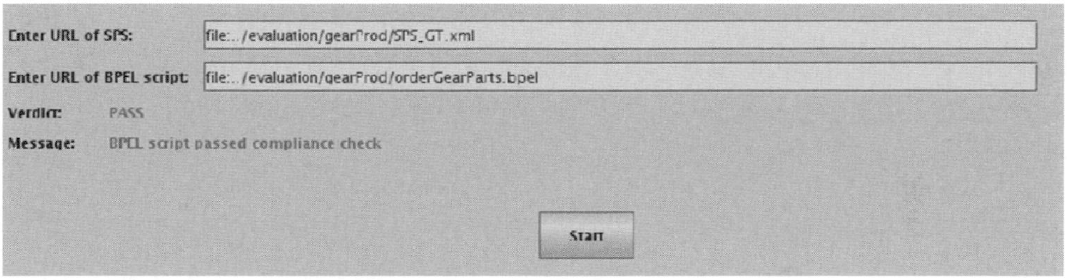

Enter URL of SPS: file:../evaluation/gearProd/SPS_GT.xml

Enter URL of BPEL script: file:../evaluation/gearProd/orderGearParts.bpel

Verdict: PASS

Message: BPEL script passed compliance check

Start

Figure 20: Successful Assessment of BPEL Script in Prototype

Without executing the BPEL script, the prototype inspects it step by step to ensure that the restrictions specified in the SPS are obeyed. If any violation is detected, the program stops its analysis and returns a FAIL verdict. It also indicates the location in the BPEL script giving rise to this verdict together with the restriction in the SPS violated at that location. If the inspection is completed without detecting any violation of the SPS, then the prototype assigns a PASS verdict to the BPEL script.

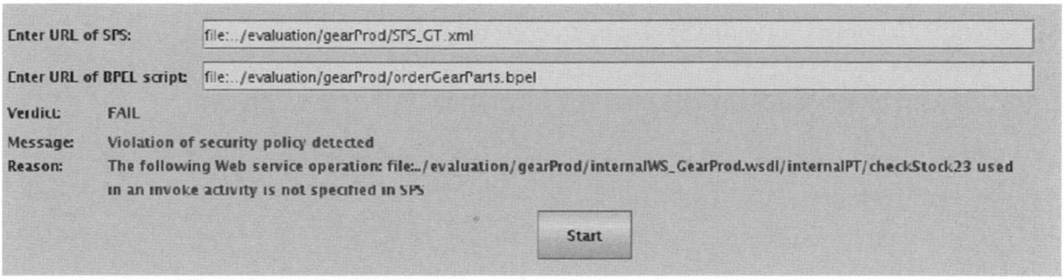

Enter URL of SPS: file:../evaluation/gearProd/SPS_GT.xml

Enter URL of BPEL script: file:../evaluation/gearProd/orderGearParts.bpel

Verdict: FAIL

Message: Violation of security policy detected

Reason: The following Web service operation: file:../evaluation/gearProd/internalWS_GearProd.wsdl/internalPT/checkStock23 used in an invoke activity is not specified in SPS

Start

Figure 21: Detection of SPS Violation in Prototype

7.4.1 Conversion of SPS into Internal Representation

When the prototype is started via the "Start" button, it reads the XML document containing the SPS and converts it into an internal representation. To this purpose, the SPS document is parsed using a DOM parser returning the structure of the XML as a whole. By processing this structure step by step, the program creates internal representations for the Web services indicated in the SPS. For each restricted

162 Chinnici *et al.*, 2007

internal or external Web service (elements `<iwsrs>` and `<ewsrs>`, respectively) found in the SPS, an instance of class `CSPSRestIntWs` or `CSPSRestExtWs`, respectively, is created to contain the name and port type along with the restrictions with respect to the input and output parameters applicable to each Web service. For each unrestricted internal or external Web service (elements `<unrestrIntWs>` and `<unrestrExtWs>`, respectively), an instance of the classes `CSPSUnrestIntWs` or `CSPSUnrestExtWs`, respectively, is created to contain just the name and port type of these Web services.

7.4.2   Conversion of Variable Declarations into Internal Representation

After parsing the SPS and converting it into an internal representation, the XML document containing the BPEL script is parsed. Unlike the parsing of the SPS, the BPEL script is parsed using a SAX parser since this type of XML parser returns the document element by element, which has been found to be better suited for stepping through the BPEL script. For each declaration of a variable encountered, the program creates an instance of class `CbpelVariable` that contains the name of the variable, its message type along with the corresponding name space and all parts within this message type. The parts within a message type are determined by parsing the WSDL definition in which this message type is specified. For the purpose of the prototype it is assumed that the URI indicated in the name space reference with the message type is a direct reference to the file containing the WSDL definition. It should be noted that, in general, such URIs need not to be direct references to files but may also contain some sort of indirect references that have to be resolved first to get access to the WSDL definition. Since such resolution of URIs is not essential for the proof of concept, it has not been implemented but only direct file references have been supported in the prototype.

7.4.3   Combined Forward/Backward Information Flow Analysis

One of the main tasks of the prototype is the information flow analysis both in forward and backward directions to decide whether restrictions of class 3 and class 6 would be obeyed by the BPEL script checked. In order to avoid repeated parsing of the BPEL script, the variables as being the containers of the information to be passed in outbound messages to so-called partners of a BPEL script and received in inbound messages from these partners have been designed to be represented in a special manner. Besides accommodating the content representing the information stored in these variables, the internal representation of variables has been designed to also encompass both the restrictions associated with the particular information as found in the corresponding SPS (*i.e.*, visibility restriction with or without target relaxation) and the source the information was gained from. This way, whenever an information contained in a variable is to be included in an outbound message of an `invoke` activity or a `reply` activity, it can be checked whether visibility restrictions are obeyed and, in case an input parameter of the Web service invoked is subject to source restriction (class 6), it can be determined whether the source of this information complies to this restriction. By collecting all restrictions implied to an output parameter of a Web service in the variable that accepts this parameter along with its name and the value returned by the Web service, information flow analysis may be performed in forward and backward direction by just evaluating this additional content beyond the pure value of the variable.

As an example, the treatment of a Web service invocation is described in further detail. As this treatment is the most complex one in the assessment since all types of restrictions may apply, describing the steps performed gives an overview of the actions performed by the prototype with any BPEL activity.

Upon encountering an `invoke` activity, the prototype determines the Web service invoked and looks up the internal representation of the SPS for the information present therein for the specific Web service. If the Web service is not found in the SPS, the processing stops because invocation of a Web service not defined in SPS as being allowed represents a violation of the security policy. Remember that for every Web service that is allowed to be invoked an entry in the SPS has to exist as stated in Chapter 5.

If the Web service is found in SPS, the restrictions defined there are copied for further use. Since the output parameters of a Web service invocation are stored in a variable defined in the BPEL script, the restrictions contained in the `<output>` element corresponding to the particular Web service are stored in the instance of the class `CBpelVariable` representing this variable. Along with the restrictions, the URI of the Web service invoked is stored in this variable for potential later use in validating potential source restrictions (class 6).

Usually, this process of storing the restrictions for the output part of a Web service in the variable receiving this output will override the information stored there with former uses of this variable in Web service invocations. However, if the Web service invocation was found in an (actual or potential) parallel flow (*i.e.*, within a flow, switch,[163] or pick activity), then the information does not override the information already stored there but a special treatment of information flow analysis in parallel flows applies as will be described in Section 7.4.4.

The variable used as input message to the Web service invoked is analysed with respect to the accumulated restrictions already stored in it. In this way it is checked whether visibility restricted (class 3) information is contained in the variable to determine whether conflicts with those restrictions would occur by passing this information to the current Web service. In the case that class 6 restrictions are present for the input parameters of a Web service, the origin of the information contained

---

163 Remember that the prototype was based on a previous version of BPEL. The **switch** activity has been replaced by the **if** activity in the latest version of BPEL providing essentially the same functionality.

in the variable will be used to assess compliance or detect potential non-compliance with these class 6 restrictions.

Similar processing as with the input and output parameters in an `invoke` activity applies to the `reply` and `receive` activities (and the receiving parts in a `pick` activity), respectively.

7.4.4 Handling of Parallel Flows in Information Flow Analysis

If an assignment of a message returned by an invoke activity or a receive activity is encountered within an (actual or potential) parallel flow in the BPEL script, the information stored in the variable will not be overridden. Instead, the information to be stored in the variable is labelled with a hierarchical flow identifier enabling simultaneous collection of information related to all (potential) parallel information flows. This way, the backward information flow analysis can use the restrictions from all former parallel information flows. If information from parallel flows is present and the same variable is re-used as container for the output of a Web service, the hierarchical flow identifiers stored with the information has to be considered to decide which part of the information to override and which to keep.

7.4.5 Implementation of Covert Channel Prevention

In order to prevent covert channels[164], the prototype takes a rigorous approach in disallowing any visibility restricted information to be used for flow control purposes (*i.e.*, in the activities `exit`, `throw`, `wait`, `compensateScope`, `while`, `repeat-Until`, `switch`,[163] `forEach`, and the timeout part of `pick`) or in a `validate` activity (or assign activity with attribute `validate="true"`). Remember that only the `switch` activity is actually implemented in the prototype. However, the same processing as implemented for the `switch` activity would also apply for covert channel detection if the prototype is to be amended to also support these other activities.

Whenever such an activity is encountered during parsing the BPEL script, the prototype checks whether any variable is used in this activity. If not, then the activity is considered uncritical with respect to covert channel establishment. However, if a variable is detected in such an activity, then it is checked in the information flow history of this variable whether it contains visibility-restricted information (class 3 restriction) or may contain such information from potential parallel flows. If that is the case, then a violation of the restrictions in the SPS is assumed without further analysis whether the further processing actually would exhibit observable behaviour that is influenced by the visibility-restricted information in such a manner that conclusion on this information could be drawn.

---

164 cf., Sabelfeld and Myers, 2003

This rigorous approach to covert channel prevention may be too strict in some instances, but it assures in any case that no BPEL script with undiscovered covert channels will pass the compliance assessment. If refusal based on falsely supposed covert channels because of this rigorous approach would be an issue then more sophisticated algorithms for differentiating between harmless and harmful use of visibility-restricted information in flow control would be required. For instance, a more sophisticated approach for covert channel prevention could try to analyse whether the externally observable behaviour would be distinguishably different depending on the information used in these activities for flow control purposes. One should bear in mind that such analysis is complex and increases the risk to overlook a covert channel that was possibly included in disguise. Therefore, the strict approach for covert channel prevention currently taken should only be weakened if urgent needs would require doing so. Even under these circumstances, utmost care has to be taken not to overdo this relaxation of the rules for covert channel prevention.

7.5 Evaluation of Prototype

The prototype has been evaluated in order to investigate whether the algorithms defined for performing the different checks required during compliance assessment of a BPEL script are capable of distinguishing allowed and disallowed semantics expressed by it. For this purpose, variants of BPEL scripts for the `control` process of the example in Figure 4 have been subject to an automated security assessment processing simulated by the prototype. The scope of this evaluation has been concentrated on the aspect, to which extent machine-based analysis of compliance with security policies defined in terms of security-relevant semantic patterns of BPEL scripts may be performed without human assistance. In particular, the reliability of machine-based assessment statements as to compliance with security policies was evaluated. In addition, syntax checking of SPS implemented in the prototype and the issued error messages in the case of syntax error detection were tested.

Listing 7: Extract from BPEL Script Invoking WS not Defined in SPS

```
<invoke  partnerLink="gearProd"
         portType="int:internalPT"
         operation="checkStock23"
         inputVariable="gearProducerCheckInput"
         outputVariable="gearProducerCheckOutput" />
```

The BPEL script and SPS examples used for evaluation purposes were chosen based on the CBP example in Figure 4. The BPEL scripts were supposed to define the `control` business process and the SPS to contain the restrictions with respect to Web service invocation as discussed in Chapter 2. BPEL scripts with the following characteristics were used:

- BPEL script completely complying to SPS (example outcome depicted in Figure 20)
- BPEL script invoking Web service not contained in SPS (example outcome depicted in Figure 21 with the BPEL snippet containing the violation depicted in Listing 7 where invalid WS operation is typed in red)
- BPEL script passing visibility-restricted information to external Web service (not indicated in target relaxation)
- BPEL script passing information to source-restricted input message to a Web service where source of information passed does not comply to source restriction
- BPEL script using visibility-restricted information in branch condition of a `switch` activity

Evaluation of the prototype using these BPEL examples proved successful. The outcome of running the prototype with the particular BPEL script as input indicated the SPS violation intentionally introduced in the script. From these results and the considerations with respect to coverage of the prototype in Section 7.1, it could be concluded that implementing a procedure for automatic compliance assessment of BPEL scripts with security policies specified using the XML schema described in Section 7.2.2 was feasible and the implementation of the assessment procedure as described in Section 0 based on a class hierarchy as proposed in Section 7.3 turned out to be comparatively straightforward.

By implementing selected parts of a compliance assessment procedure based on the methods described in Chapters 5 and 6, it could be shown that the novel approach presented in previous chapters is suited for automatic compliance assessment. Having only realised part of the assessment procedure in the prototype does not reduce the evidence gained because the discussion in Section 7.1 has clarified that the selection of functionality covered the main aspects of this procedure. One aspect of functionality considered crucial for the automatic performance of compliance assessment is the information flow analysis in forward and backward direction while checking a BPEL script for possible violations of security policy. The essential basis for this information flow analysis has been realised in the prototype by storing the restrictions imposed to information gained from Web service invocations together with the source of an information item in the internal representations of the variables storing the information.

Furthermore, as assembled in Table 4, the way to implement the missing parts of the functionality either can be deduced from the already implemented parts or is straightforward to realise such that no template for its implementation is required. However, even though the prototype made clear that the construction of a compliance assessment tool covering the whole range of BPEL is feasible and introduced data structures and algorithms appropriate to serve as templates for the missing functionality, it should be noted that the overall effort for building such a tool in product quality would require a significant effort.

7.6 Summary

The proof of concept of the approach to compliance assessment of BPEL scripts with local security policy of the executing site has been conducted by a prototype implementing essential aspects of the compliance assessment procedure. Though the prototype was not aimed at implementing the full range of functionality of this procedure, it has shown that all kinds of checking required in the course of compliance assessment have either been covered by the prototype, are easy to be covered by straightforward amendment of functionally already implemented, or are straightforward to implement and would add nothing to the proof of concept.

Only in the case, the rigorous approach to covert channel prevention adopted with all other activities prone to covert channels would be deemed not acceptable for the `validate` activity newly added to the BPEL standard, more sophisticated checking for covert channel prevention would be required that are not yet covered by the prototype and cannot be considered straightforward amendments of functionality already implemented. However, these checks may be also implemented without posing essential problems. An outline of the procedure required to perform this type of checking for potential covert channels associated with the `validate` activity is included in Appendix 2.

During establishing the XML schema for the machine-readable specification of the SPS and the initial design for the prototype based on the example of a CBP in Figure 4, several new insights have been gained that gave rise to adapting the XML schema and led to amendments of the approach described in Chapters 4 through 6. The following modifications of the initial approach were induced by the development of the prototype:

- The need to provide target relaxation (*i.e.*, allow visibility-restricted information to be sent to specific targets external to the local domain) has been recognised during the attempt to establish an SPS for the example in Figure 4. The capability to specify such target relaxation was not included in initial versions of the approach[165].
- In the same context, the need was recognised to extend the definition of the class 4 restriction that was initially defined to only encompass input parameters forbidden to be used. Since such a restriction can only be applied to optional input parameters of a Web service, the reverse restriction had to be added for completeness, that is, the requirement that a value for an optional parameter

---

165 Fischer *et al.*, 2006

has always to be passed to avoid an eventual default value (or default mechanism) for such a parameter to take effect.

- Further it turned out during the design of the prototype to be necessary to not only allow for one instance of SPS for a particular pair of business partners exchanging BPEL scripts for remote execution, but also provide the capability for having different SPS instances depending on different application contexts in which these partners may perform collaborative business processes. Such instances would typically allow for different sets of restrictions on Web service invocations (allowing different Web services to be invoked or having deviating restrictions on common subsets of Web services present in different SPSs).

The description of the results in Chapters 4 through 6 is based on the amendments added as consequences of these insights.

The viability of further proposals made in previous chapters such as approaches for the delegation of the compliance assessment or for coping with the requirement for dynamic checking in pre-execution assessment of compliance is deemed to be given as granted from its description in the book without further requirements for proof of concept. Therefore, providing exemplary implementations thereof was not considered necessary to confirm their feasibility, but would only have resulted in increased efforts spent for software development without contributing new insights.

Having now presented the results achieved for the field of CBPs, the next chapter considers possible application of these results to related fields. Since also based on BPEL scripts, Grid processes defined on top of Grid services as well as Cloud processes or workflows defined on top of Web services have proven particularly suited for such wider application of the results achieved.

8 Extending Results to Grid and Cloud Computing

In this chapter, the results achieved in the field of business processes are investigated with respect to their transferability to other fields where comparable circumstances prevail. The chapter has been included in this book to demonstrate that the techniques developed in the previous chapters for the CBP context can be generalised to also be applicable in related fields. Showing their applicability in a wider context is deemed to further the validity of the approach presented.

The fields of Grid computing and Cloud computing have been adopted for this purpose due to evident similarities to business processes. Readers particularly interested in this extension of the methods and procedures introduced for the field of CBP may directly skip to this chapter after having read Chapters 4 and 5.

In Grid processes, Grid services[166] play a role similar to Web services in the field of business processes. Therefore, BPEL also has found its way to application in Grid context for the specification of long-running processes modelled with BPEL invoking Grid services[167].

Because of its analogy to using BPEL in collaborative business process (CBP) context, trying a transfer of the results on security policy enforcement for remotely defined business processes as presented in the former chapters to a Grid process context was suggesting itself. Therefore, it was tried to transfer the method of defining security policies in terms of security-relevant semantics inherent in BPEL in order to facilitate the assessment of compliance with such policies from the field of business processes to the Grid context. The discussion evaluates the extent to which this is successful, and where limitations and issues for further study exist.

In situations where workflows are defined in a Cloud computing context by the use of BPEL scripts and orchestration is achieved by invocation of services similar to Web services, conditions are similar enough to anticipate that results transferred to Grid processes can be equally adopted to be applied to Cloud context. Therefore, the propositions made in this chapter for Grid processes are deemed to be also valid for such situations in Cloud computing without always mentioning this explicitly in the following. In his PhD thesis, Höing[168] discusses such BPEL-based workflows in Grid and Cloud contexts with respect to security aspects. In Cloud context, he refers to services used for orchestration of workflows as Cloud services, obviously in analogy to Grid services in Grid context. The term Cloud service,

---

166 Tuecke *et al.*, 2003
167 *e.g.*, Amnuaykanjanasin and Nupairoj 2005; Gannon *et al.*, 2005
168 Höing, 2010

however, is used by other authors[169] differently. They use this term to refer to the Cloud computing offering of a provider such as Amazon's Elastic Compute Cloud[170] or Google's App Engine[171].

In Cloud context, different delivery models for providing Cloud computing are considered and categorised depending on the degree of integration of hardware and software in the service offering[172]. Infrastructure as a service (IaaS), platform as a service (PaaS), and software as a service (SaaS) are typical terms that are used to refer to such categories for service offerings in Cloud computing[173]. Anstett *et al.*[164] investigate how BPEL can be used in different delivery models for outsourcing processes. They also discuss security challenges implied by the different ways of outsourcing. In Section 8.6, it will be discussed to which extend the approaches introduced here for assessing BPEL-defined processes with respect to their compliance to security policies will be applicable also to scenarios where BPEL is used in different Cloud delivery models.

A further aspect addressed herein is the possibility to delegate the task of assessing compliance of BPEL-defined Grid processes with local security policies. This aspect might be of minor interest in the Cloud context and, therefore, is considered here only in the Grid context. In principle, however, the approaches proposed here could be equally applied to the Cloud context if appropriate requests should exist. An infrastructure supporting the delegation of this task to one or several dedicated nodes in a network or to specific assessment centres has also been introduced for the CBP context (cf. Section 6.3). This possibility may be of even more interest in the Grid context where typically many small to medium size computers are involved, spread over different locations, and not necessarily belonging to a larger organisation (as typically encountered in a CBP context) that can afford or provide the effort required for the task of performing the security policy assessment as proposed in this chapter.

8.1   Motivation for Remote Definition of Grid Processes

In order to motivate why remote definition of a BPEL-based Grid process may be sensible, a typical scenario of Grid service execution is considered. In Figure 22, a provider of processing resources is supposed to operate a BPEL-enabled platform. On this platform, Grid processes defined by BPEL scripts are running that invoke Grid services provided by a variety of service providers and offering enhanced Grid services to service requestors in different roles (roles A and B in the example

---

169   *e.g.*, Anstett *et. al.*, 2009
170   http://aws.amazon.com
171   http://appengine.google.com
172   Aymerich *et al.*, 2008
173   Anstett *et al.*,2009

of Figure 22). In a CBP context, availability of BPEL-enabled platforms at every site involved in such a business process could be assumed, since this already is or soon will be common practice in enterprises engaging in CBPs. Therefore, gaining access to a BPEL-enabled node was not considered a motivation for remotely defining BPEL scripts. Instead, location-dependent access restrictions gave rise to defining business processes displaced from the intended location of execution. In a Grid context, however, the lack of access to a BPEL-enabled platform could very well motivate definition of BPEL scripts for remote execution since not every location having the need for defining Grid processes may be assumed to have local access to a BPEL-enabled platform. In particular, having (local) access to such a platform may not be considered a standard situation in small or medium-sized organisations. Therefore, defining BPEL scripts for remote execution might be an interesting amendment of current state of the art of using BPEL in a Grid context.

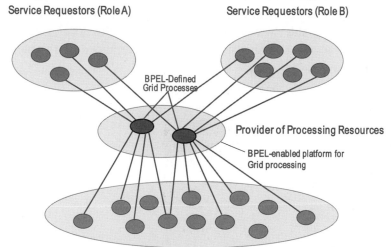

Figure 22: Grid Process Execution Scenario

A further motivation for acceptance of remotely defined BPEL scripts in Grid processing could be the reduction of maintenance overhead that can be gained this way. Consider the situation depicted in Figure 23. Here it is assumed that one particular service requestor in role A, say service requestor A1, would have special requirements differing from the rest of service requestors within role A. These requirements could be accomplished by creating a variant of an existing Grid service on the platform of the Grid processing provider that would, for instance, invoke Grid services differently. As long as only one such variant would be required, the additional maintenance overhead for modifying the existing Grid process and operating the variant for service requestor A1 may be moderate and, therefore, be acceptable for the platform operator. However, if an increasing number of service requestors have special requirements that would also lead to variants of existing Grid processes on the platform, the effort for the definition and maintenance of a large amount of variants may no longer be affordable for the platform operator. Therefore, the platform operator could allow that the different service requestors having requirements deviating from the main stream of the service requestors in a particular role (role A in this example) perform the modifications of BPEL scripts on their own and send the modified BPEL script to the Grid processing provider for execution of the Grid process defined by this script. In this way, the effort for the definition of the modified BPEL script and its maintenance in case of changing requirements would be moved to the requestor of the modified Grid service, thereby relieving the platform operator from this effort. As in the CBP context, such definition of BPEL scripts remotely from the location of execution is technically feasible because of the nature of BPEL being a standardised process definition language.

However, in a similar way as with remotely defined BPEL-based business processes, security issues may impede practical application of this approach with BPEL-defined Grid processes. Being able to assess the compliance with local security policies prior to execution would decisively increase the acceptance of remotely defined BPEL scripts for execution, though.

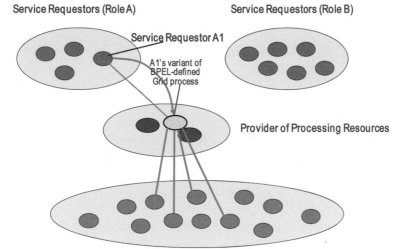

Figure 23: Reducing Maintenance Overhead by Remote Definition of Grid Processes

Making otherwise inaccessible Web services available to a controlling business process while still observing the security policy with respect to non-disclosure of information gained or access to resources granted by invoking such Web services was one motivation for remote definition of business processes in the CBP context. Since the conditions to be observed with respect to access control could be much more diverse in a Grid context[174], the investigation of generally granting access to

---

174 Chadwick *et al.*, 2006

otherwise restricted Grid services as the reason for executing remotely defined BPEL scripts is left to further study.

However, the transfer of the results from the CBP context to the Grid context seems to be most obvious for situations where Grid technology is used for forming virtual organisations (VOs)[175]. In this context, the number of partners are limited and controlled by regulations for joining a VO, particularly with respect to authentication and authorization. If remotely defined BPEL scripts are used for controlling Grid processes in VOs, there are many analogies to business processes defined by remotely defined BPEL scripts in the CBP context. As with CBPs, local security policies of an organisation offering resources for being used in a VO usually determine access to these resources. These policies will result in restrictions to allowed semantics of remotely defined BPEL scripts that may be accepted for execution from a member of the VO. Such restrictions on allowed semantics may further restrict access to Grid services than access would be restricted by security policies of the sites offering these services alone. Reasons for this could be that allowing invocation of a Grid service in a particular context of a Grid process would violate a security policy such as prevention of generating or relaying mass e-mail from within the domain executing the BPEL script.

Before the transfer of the results presented in previous chapters is addressed, a comparison is drawn between the situations in CBP context and Grid context, as summarised in Table 5. With respect to the participants of a CBP or Grid process, the number is small and tends to be constant over time in the CBP context while in the Grid context this number is larger and tends to vary over time. The number of Web processes possibly involved in a CBP tends to be small whereas the number of potentially involved Grid services may be large. In the CBP context, the location of a Web service matters, that means that it will be differentiated whether a Web service is provided locally in the domain executing the business process or externally either within the domain of the invoker of the business process or in other domains.

The motivation for remote definition of BPEL scripts in the Grid process are the reduction of coordination overhead when modification of the CBP is required, while in the Grid context the reduction of complexity in maintaining lots of diverging modifications for different service requestors may motivate the acceptance or remotely defined Grid processes. Furthermore, allowing access to otherwise inaccessible resources or information in a controlled manner may also motivate remote definition of BPEL scripts in the CBP context whereas in the Grid context increasing the flexibility for Grid process specification and offering access to BPEL-enabled platforms may additionally motivate remote definition of BPEL scripts. The security policies in the CBP context may predominantly be focussed on the

---

175 Foster *et al.*, 2001

protection of information and resources against unauthorised disclosure or use. In contrast, protection against misuse or excessive use of processing resources or, in general, protection of the processing platform offered by a provider against exploitation to perform Grid processes with unreasonable or undue behaviour may amount to the main objective of security policies.

Table 5: Comparison Between CBP Context and Grid Context

Aspect	CPB Context	Grid Context
Participants of a CBP/Grid process	Small in number and tends to be constant over time	Comparatively large in number and tends to vary over time
Number of Web/ Grid services potentially involved	Comparatively small	Tends to be high
Location of Web/Grid services	Differentiated between local and external Web service (wrt executing site)	Location of Grid services tends to be irrelevant
Motivation for remote definition of BPEL scripts	Reduction of coordination overhead (time) if modification of CBP is required	Reduction of maintenance overhead (complexity) if diverging modifications are required
	Allowing controlled access to otherwise inaccessible resources (typically internal services of executing domain)	Increasing flexibility in Grid process specification
		Offering access to BPEL-enabled processing resources
Main focus of security policies	Protection of information and resources against unauthorised disclosure or use	Protection against misuse or excessive use of processing resources (prevention of unreasonable or undue behaviour)

8.2   Approaches to Specification of Grid Service Security

Since security in the Grid context plays a paramount role, much research has been dedicated to this field on Grid computing. In particular, research concerned with expressing security policies in the context of VOs are related to the approach presented herein. Detsch *et al.*[176], for example, proposed a security architecture for

---

176   Detsch *et al.*, 2004

peer-to-peer-based Grid computing where a security layer offering security-related functionality resides between the Grid application layer and the communication infrastructure. In this way, applications do not need to implement such functionality on their own. Security requirements may be stated by each member of a VO on a peer-by-peer basis or for groups of peers.

Welch *et al.*[177] have investigated how security functionality can be made available to Grid services, in particular in the context of VOs. A security model for Open Grid Services Architecture (OGSA)[178] specifying security services to provide different security functionality is proposed for this purpose. The authors show how security-related specifications from the field of Web services can be used in the context of this security architecture. In their paper, expressing security policies for using a Web service in terms of WS-Policy specifications[179] and publishing these policies together with the WSDL specification[180] of the service is also addressed.

It should be noted that security policy expressed in terms of WS-Policy deals with the requirements for security mechanisms to be applied or provided for using a Grid service (such as certificates to be required for accessing a service, or encryption methods to be applied when communicating input and output parameters of a service). In a layered architecture as in Figure 1, these mechanisms are to be provided in layers below the business process layer as already discussed in Section 3.1.4. The security policies expressed in the two approaches above, therefore, address aspects of policies complementary to those that have to be obeyed in the business process layer if remotely defined BPEL scripts are to be executed.

8.3 Security-Relevant Semantic Patterns in BPEL-Based Grid Processes

In order to transfer the results of the analysis of security-relevant semantics of BPEL as a specification language (cf. Chapter 4) to the Grid context, the classes of security policy-induced access restrictions discussed in Section 4.3 (cf. Table 1) are reconsidered here with respect to Grid services (GS) as shown in Table 6.

Compared to Table 1, the term 'Web service' had to be replaced by 'Grid service' throughout Table 6. Apart from that, most descriptions could be transferred otherwise unchanged (classes 1, 2, 4, and 5) or nearly unchanged (class 6). Only the description of class 3 was modified to better fit in the Grid context and a new class 7 was introduced.

177   Welch *et al.*, 2003
178   Foster *et al.*, 2002
179   Bajaj *et al.*, 2006
180   Chinnici *et al.*, 2007

While in the CBP context the restriction in class 3 was specified in terms of restricted visibility to targets outside the domain executing a BPEL script, this distinction does not always play an important role in the Grid context. Therefore, the definition of class 3 was abstracted from the location where a target resides to generally express restricted information flow to dedicated targets irrespective of their location. Hence, restrictions will be specified in terms of specific Grid services or particular input parameters thereof that are forbidden to receive the values returned from these parameters. In order, for instance, to prevent a list of e-mail addresses returned by a particular Grid service to be used for generating mass e-mail, this output parameter could be restricted not to be used as input parameter of particular other Grid services known to generate an e-mail to each address passed to it. Obviously, the location of the second Grid service (inside or outside the executing site) does not matter in this case.

Table 6: Classification of Access Restrictions to Grid Services and GS Parameters

Class	Description of Restriction
1	Grid service with unrestricted access to all parts of resources or information offered
2	Grid service with completely restricted access (*i.e.*, Grid service that are not allowed to be invoked)
3	Output parameter of a Grid service with restricted visibility of values returned with respect to specific targets: information returned by these parameters is not allowed to be carried to specific targets (*i.e.*, to specific other Grid service or to particular parameters of specific Grid service)
4	Optional input parameter of a Grid service with usage restrictions in two different embodiments: a) optional parameter not allowed to be used b) optional parameter always required
5	Input parameter of a Grid service with constrained set of values allowed: input parameters may only be used with particular values from a subset of the values allowed by the syntactic definition of this parameter
6	Input parameter of a Grid service with values restricted to specific sources: only values from particular origins may be used, for instance, only values returned by a particular Grid service or a specific parameter of a particular Grid service
7	Grid service particularly prone to overload if invoked excessively. For these Grid service, maximum invocation rates or maximum amount of data passed to it to prevent overloading will have to be observed

Unlike in the CBP context, where effective runtime mechanisms for prevention of overloading a Web services could be deemed to be in place (in layers below the business layer) at a platform running these services, this might not, in general, be expected from sites running Grid services. Therefore, a security policy of a site accepting remotely defined BPEL scripts in a Grid context could require that a process running on resources of this site shall not cause overload (running the risk to result in an intentional or unintentional denial of service attack) to specific Grid services known to be prone to overload when invoked in a particular manner. Since, in a Grid context, effective runtime prevention of overloading a Grid service shall not be expected to take place at all sites running these services, semantic patterns of BPEL potentially causing such overload have to be identified and looked for in pre-execution compliance assessment to prevent BPEL scripts including such patterns from being executed.

Table 7: Security Relevance of Semantic Patterns with Primitive Activities (Grid)

Primitive Activities		Class 3	Class 4	Cl. 5/6	Class 7
invoke	Invocation of a Grid service	IFA(v)	u	IFA(w/s)	IFA(a)
receive	Waiting for a message to arrive	IFA(v)	–	–	–
reply	Sending a reply to a message received	–	u	IFA(w/s)	–
assign	Assignment of values between two different locations	(relevant in IFA only)			
wait	Waiting for a specified amount of time	time(v)	–	–	–
throw	Indication of exceptions such as failures during execution	except(v)	–	–	–
rethrow[*]	Forwarding of exceptions causing fault handler execution to containing scope	–	–	–	–
empty	No operation	–	–	–	–
validate	Validate values against type declaration	val(v)	–	–	–
exit	Termination of a process instance	exit(v)	–	–	–
compensate[*]	Initiate compensation as specified by compensation handlers of corresponding scope and all nesting scopes	–	–	–	–
compensate Scope[*]	Initiate compensation as specified by compensation handler of a specific scope	scope(v)	–	–	–

*	=	Activity only to be used within fault handlers
−	=	Not relevant for access control and information flow
u	=	Check that actual use complies to usage restriction of optional Grid service parameters
IFA =		Information flow analysis:

(v) with respect to visibility of values read from Grid service

(w) with respect to values written to Grid service

(s) with respect to sources of values written to Grid service

(a) with respect to amount of data written

There are two types of overload that may be caused to a Grid service. One type is sending more data in an invocation of a Grid service than can be handled. The other type is invoking a Grid service at a higher rate than this service can cope with. Therefore, performance-related restrictions related to these types of overload may be indicated for a Grid service falling in this new class 7 in the Grid context.

Table 8: Security Relevance of Semantic Patterns with Structured Activities (Grid)

Structured Activities		Class 3	Class 4	Cl. 5/6	Class 7
sequence	Definition of a fixed execution order	−	−	−	FQ
flow	Parallel execution of activities	−	−	−	FQ
if	Branching between several alternate activities depending on conditions	switch cond(v)	−	−	−
while repeat Until	Iterative execution, i.e., looping	loop cond(v)	−	−	FQ
forEach	Iterative consecutive or parallel execution	Iteration bounds(v)	−	−	FQ
		preempt(v)			PI
pick	Waiting simultaneously for several events to occur and proceeding with the event that occurs first	IFA(v)	−	−	−
		time(v)	−	−	−

−	=	Not relevant for access control and information flow
IFA(v) =		Information flow analysis with respect to visibility of values read from Grid service
FQ	=	Invocation frequency to be checked against maximum
PI	=	Check number of parallel instantiations

The security-relevant semantic patterns again being formed as combinations of BPEL activities with restriction classes of Grid service invocation as in Section 4.4 were adapted from Tables 2 and 3. While all semantic patterns identified there are also relevant in the Grid context and, therefore, could be transferred by simply substituting the term "Grid service" for "Web service", some new semantic patterns were added as combinations of BPEL activities and the new restriction class 7 in the last column of Tables 7 and 8, respectively. As indicated in this column, attention has to be paid during compliance assessment to semantic patterns identified there as being capable of generating high invocation frequencies of Grid services. This could be the case when a Grid service is invoked within while, repeat-Until, sequence, flow, or forEach activities at a high rate or with short intermediate time intervals (marked 'FQ' in Table 8) and by a high amount of parallel instantiations in the parallel version of the forEach activities (marked 'PI' in Table 8). Overloading a Grid service could also occur by passing large amount of data to Grid services not designed for coping with such data volumes in invoke activities (marked 'IFA(a)' in Table 7). With the exception of the semantic patterns formed with the new restriction class 7 which had been added here, the results of the analysis of security-relevant semantics of BPEL leads to the same results as in the CBP context.

8.4 Rewriting Security Policies to Support Pre-Execution Security Policy Assessment

As in the CBP context, rewriting security policies in terms of security-relevant semantics is also proposed for the Grid process to support compliance assessment of remotely defined BPEL-based business processes with these policies. The concept of an SPS, as introduced in Chapter 5, will also prove useful here to reflect the security policies of a specific domain. In the CBP context, such an SPS was defined domain-specific with respect to two domains, namely the domain where the security policy is in effect (*i.e.*, domain executing BPEL scripts) and the domain defining and sending BPEL scripts for execution. The XML-based schema for specifying an SPS in machine-readable form which has been the basis for implementing the prototype of an automatic assessment of BPEL scripts for compliance with security policies has been introduced in Section 7.2.

In the Grid context, since semantic patterns have been modified (definition of restriction class 3) and supplemented (patterns involving new restriction class 7) compared with those found in Section 4.4, the check list as basis of an SPS as well as the XML-based SPS schema for machine-readable versions thereof have to be modified accordingly in order to accommodate this new set of security-relevant semantic patterns.

Unlike in the CBP context, an SPS may not be sensibly defined for a specific foreign domain, since Grid computing is concerned with a potentially large amount of foreign domains that are essentially indistinguishable from the point of view of the domain executing the BPEL-defined Grid processes. However, in a VO environment, if the identities of members and their privileges to execute Grid services are known in advance, defining an SPS similar to the CBP context for each other member in the VO that is allowed to send BPEL scripts for execution could make sense.

Therefore, with the exception of the latter situation, only one or a few SPSs without any relation to a specific external domain will make sense in the Grid context. If more than one SPS will be specified for a domain, they are expected to be differentiated with respect to different application contexts for which they apply (*e.g.*, computational simulation in a particular field, collection of field-specific data such as in meteorology). Although details of application context-dependent SPSs are left to further study, it is anticipated that such SPSs will be tightly bound to access privileges or roles classifying the sender of a BPEL script.

Specifying security policies in terms of security-relevant semantic patterns identified in Section 8.3 requires an exhaustive list of all Grid services allowed to be invoked by a remotely defined BPEL script. Furthermore, for every Grid service mentioned in this list, the security-relevant semantics of the service and its parameters has to be known in order to determine the access restriction classes appropriate for each of them (cf. Table 6). This requirement may cause additional effort since specification of security-relevant semantics may not be available for Grid services in the first place.

It should be noted that unavailability of semantic specification (at least as far as security-relevant semantics is concerned) may prevent the approach proposed here from being applied. However, unavailability of such specification may also prevent the application of any other pre-execution approach to assessing compliance of Grid processes with security policies. This holds independently of both the location where a Grid process is being defined and executed, and also the manner in which the process is being specified (*i.e.*, independent of using BPEL or any other means for specifying Grid processes). In case of unavailable semantic specifications, the only way of enforcing security policies is monitoring the execution of a Grid process and interfering in cases where violations of security policy have been detected involving the known shortcomings of such approaches mentioned above. And even with approaches based on monitoring it may be required to have some knowledge of the semantics of the Grid services invoked by a Grid process in order to decide whether the invocation of a particular Grid service would violate any security policy-induced restriction or not. Therefore, also with these approaches, knowledge of the security-relevant semantics of Grid services as required for the assembly of an SPS will be required to a certain extent in order to make them applicable to Grid processes.

Some research has been concerned with describing the semantics of Grid services in order to support identification of matching Grid services for automatic Grid process orchestration[181]. Bringing the results of this research together with the

---

181 *e.g.*, Lorch *et al.*, 2003; Ren *et al.*, 2006

approach proposed in this chapter in order to define a framework for formally specifying security-relevant semantics of Grid services in terms of well-defined (maybe even standardised) categories is expected to be an interesting field of further study.

A further motivation for research in this direction could be the endeavour to facilitate specification of information flow restrictions of output parameters and value or source restrictions for input parameters with respect to particular characteristics of a Grid service by denoting particular semantics bound to this Grid service instead of particular Grid services themselves. Such semantic characteristics could be "returning lists of e-mail addresses" or "causes sending e-mails to addresses passed". Means to specify restrictions this way would eliminate the need to analyse every potentially allowed Grid service for falling into a specific restriction class if, in parallel, Grid services and their parameters would have been specified in terms of such characteristics with respect to their (security-relevant) semantics.

If such classification of Grid services would be available, then, for instance, in order to enforce a security policy of avoiding the generation of Spam emails at a Grid node, one could require that any output parameter with the semantic characteristic "returning a (potentially large) list of email addresses" must not be input to any parameter with the characteristic "causes sending e-mails to addresses passed". Specifying allowed and disallowed semantic patterns with respect to such categories instead of individual Grid services and their parameters obviously would help to shorten the content of an SPS considerably. How far this idea of categorizing Grid parameter semantics for this purpose can be successfully based on or linked with research such as work on semantic Grid services[182], semantic matchmaking of Grid service composition[183], or workflow ontology of Grid services[184] requires further investigation.

Such amendments of addressing semantic characteristics of Grid service parameters in an SPS are expected to involve increased complexity of the assessment task because of required matching of SPS and semantic characteristics of the Grid services actually used in a BPEL script. Even before such amendments are available, it is not obvious and actually will require further investigation whether the assessment of compliance with security policies specified in an SPS is similarly straightforward as it has been shown for the CBP context by implementing the prototype (cf. Chapter 7). In particular, it is expected that covering semantic patterns involving class 7 restrictions in automatic compliance assessment prior to execution will turn out to be complex or even impossible to a certain extent since this class of restrictions addresses dynamic aspects of a BPEL script that obviously are not easy

---

182 Goble and De Roure, 2002
183 Ludwig and Reyhani, 2005
184 Beco *et al.*, 2005

to be analysed in a static pre-execution assessment. However, applying the approach to cope with dynamic checking in pre-execution analysis as proposed in Section 5.4 may also help here. For instance, in order to assure that the invocation frequency of a Grid service susceptible to overload by too high an invocation rate, a Grid service could be defined that works like a delay element and this Grid service could be indicated in the SPS as required to be invoked prior to the particular susceptible Grid service.

8.5   Delegation of Security Assessment

As already discussed in Section 6.3, delegation of compliance assessment may be advantageously be applied in distributed environments in the CBP context and may occur in a variety of ways. Delegation of compliance assessment may also be made use of in the Grid context. Actually, it may make even more sense than it already made in the CBP context and additional variants are conceivable.

Assessment can be performed against locally defined SPS (*i.e.*, SPS specified by site executing BPEL script) or against remotely defined SPS (*i.e.*, SPS specified by site defining BPEL script). The latter was not considered to be sensible in the CBP context. Such remotely defined SPS may be sent by the defining site together with the BPEL script as a kind of assertion what the business process defined by the BPEL script is going to do or not to do with respect to security-relevant semantics inherent in BPEL and the business services involved. If this approach is taken, means for checking the correspondence of the SPS and the BPEL script (*i.e.*, SPS belongs to BPEL script and both are not tampered in any way) may be provided based on appropriate certificates added to both the BPEL script and the SPS.

A remotely defined SPS provided with a BPEL script may be checked against local security policy requirements (*i.e.*, whether indications made in SPS fulfil these requirements or not). After positive assessment of compliance with these requirements, the local site

- may decide to trust in the assertion provided by the remote site and, after checking integrity and congruence of BPEL script and SPS, execute the BPEL script without any further compliance assessment, or
- may initiate an assessment of compliance in any way mentioned below.

In any of these cases, assessment of compliance with security policies expressed in an SPS may be performed in different ways as follows:

- Locally at the executing site. The potential problem with this approach as already indicated above could be that performing security policy assessment locally might be too elaborate a task to be conducted by small footprint computers (*e.g.*, stand-alone personal computers) or small organisations that cannot afford specific checking tools or acquire specific skill required for this task.

- Remotely (in an assessment centre) on behalf of the site executing the BPEL script. The SPS will be sent together with the BPEL script to the trusted assessment centre for checking compliance of BPEL script and SPS-defined security policies. In case of a centrally defined SPS, a reference to this centrally defined SPS may be sent instead of the SPS itself. The results will be returned to the executing site as certified verdicts (*i.e.*, passed or failed, the latter possibly accompanied by the reason(s) for this verdict).

- (Not applicable for locally defined SPS) Remotely (in an assessment centre) on behalf of the site defining the BPEL script with respect to an SPS defined by the remote site or centrally defined. BPEL script and SPS are sent to the assessment centre as in the previous case. The results of the assessment may be certified by the assessment centre and sent back to the defining site together with the certified (with respect to integrity and identity) BPEL script and SPS. The defining site may then pass the certified BPEL script and SPS to the executing site possibly accompanied by the certified results from the assessment centre. If an assessment centre adheres to a published policy to only certify BPEL scripts and SPSs that received a passed verdict when checked for compliance, then sending the result from the defining site to the executing site can be abandoned since, in this case, having a certificate from such an assessment centre implies the passed verdict for the BPEL script.

From the current point of view, these alternatives for performing security assessment of remotely defined BPEL scripts seem to be versatile enough to cover the requirements in the Grid context and, therefore, there seems to be no particular need for further research in this area.

8.6 Security Policy Enforcement for BPEL Processes in Cloud Delivery Models

Anstett *et al.*[185] discuss the use of BPEL as an orchestration language for processes in different Cloud delivery models, namely IaaS, PaaS, and SaaS. They also investigate security requirements to be met by BPEL engines and data base management system (DBMS), in particular, with respect to multi-tenancy in Cloud computing. They consider security requirements from the point of view of a customer in these three Cloud delivery models, Implicitly, they thereby address mechanisms for security policy enforcement in Cloud context. The authors determine the following risks and approaches to avoid them:

- With IaaS, there are no particular security issues when running BPEL-defined processes in this Cloud delivery model since the only difference to running such processes in a traditional on-premise model is the fact that the hardware is not owned by the customer, but rented from the Cloud provider.

---

185 Anstett *et al.*, 2009

- With PaaS, when running BPEL-defined processes at the platform middleware provided by the Cloud provider, this middleware also includes a BPEL engine and the DBMS. Given that the BPEL engine and the DBMS is no longer under the sole control of the customer, protecting the customer's assets as reflected by the process model and process instances needs special attention[186]. They point out that care has to be taken to avoid derivation of the underlying process model from the BPEL scripts, alteration of these scripts without detection, or execution of the scripts on another engine that could be manipulated or corrupted. As a measure of choice against these threats, the authors propose so-called obfuscated processes that are encrypted processes only executable on a particular BPEL engine. To enable this, using a public key infrastructure to ensure confidentiality and integrity of the BPEL scripts transferred from the customer to this particular engine is proposed. As further points of attack to deduce the process logic that is to be protected against unauthorised disclosure, the authors point out the DBMS storing information of the process model and process instances and audit logs or event logs. The latter could be used to reconstruct process models with workflow mining methods[187]. Protecting against such attacks by the use of private key-based encryption incurs the risk of considerably detracting data base performance unless customers have carefully balanced between parts that require protection and parts that can remain unprotected for the sake of performance. In summary, Anstett *et al.* [188] conclude that there is a considerable amount of security threats with BPEL in PaaS which only partially can be avoided by elaborate counter-measures and, therefore, trust has to be established between the customer and the Cloud provider, for instance, by having the provider's platform been certified as secure by using appropriately secured hardware and software.

- With SaaS, not only hardware and platform middleware, but also the processes are offered by the Cloud provider. Therefore, the processes are no longer considered an asset of the respective customer that needs to be protected against unauthorised disclosure. Unless a single-tenant architecture is in use that would imply a separate BPEL engine and DBMS for each customer (or tenant), measures have to be provided on order to protect the business processes and their data against unintended or unauthorised access by the Cloud provider or other tenants' processes[189]. Since multi-tenancy is one of the typical characteristics and advantages of SaaS, single-tenant architectures can be considered unusual. Therefore, Anstett *et al.* discuss several approaches to physically or logically isolate the process data of the different tenants from each other. Since the complete

---

186 *ibid.*, p. 673
187 van der Aaalst *et al.*, 2004; Agrawal *et al.*, 1998
188 Anstett *et al.*, 2009, p. 674
189 *ibid.*, p. 675

process environment from the hardware to the application is maintained by the SaaS provider, all measures described to cope with security policy enforcement are the responsibility of the provider. Also in this context, trust between the customer and the provider has to be established that the appropriate measures are set in place, for instance, by defining promised security features in a service level agreement (SLA) between the provider and the customer.

As can be seen from this overview, the requirements with respect to security in Cloud computing are various and differ with the Cloud delivery model and the point of view (customer or provider). While Anstett *et al.* only have considered security requirements from the point of view of a customer, security requirements from the point of view of a provider with respect to execution of BPEL-defined processes are as follows:

- With IaaS, the provider only offers infrastructure such as hardware to the customers. Whether they use this infrastructure for running a BPEL engine or other software is transparent to the provider. His only interest is that the customers make use of this infrastructure in a way and possibly up to a certain extent that has been agreed upon in advance. Therefore, particular security issues with running BPEL-defined processes does not exist for the provider,

- With PaaS, the provider offering a BPEL-enabled platform to his customers is in a fairly similar situation as the Grid provider in Section 8.1. Therefore, the considerations made for transferability of methods introduced for CBPs in Chapters 4 to 6 to the Grid context also apply here. Also the extension to overload prevention introduced and discussed for the Grid context in Section 8.3 may be of interest in this delivery model. In addition, the provider can make the SPS part of his SLA with his customers if he wants to control the way how customers make use of the BPEL engine, in particular with respect to using resource intensive services. The provider could apply the compliance assessment procedures as described in Chapter 6 based on the SPS laid down in the SLA with the customer for every BPEL-defined process submitted by the customer for execution by the BPEL engine contained in the PaaS offering of the provider.

  If obfuscated processes as proposed by Anstett *et al.*[190] are in use, however, extensions of the procedure for compatibility assessment of BPEL-defined processes and security policies are required to make the encrypted processes readable for the assessment procedure.

- With SaaS, the provider delivers the application as a whole to his customers or tenants including any BPEL-defined processes possibly required in this application. Therefore, the provider is not in the situation to accept remotely defined BPEL scripts for execution at his platform. The only way an SaaS provider could make use of the methods described for CBPs and Grid processes would be to incorporate them into his measures for quality assurance in developing new or

---

190 Anstett *et al.* 2009, p. 673

adapting existing software provided to his tenants. In this case, the security policy to be enforced would be the one of the provider, possibly amended by tenant-dependent aspects if tenant-specific processes are to be provided

From the point of view of a customer, only the customer of IaaS could sensibly make use of the methods proposed in the previous chapters for the CBP context because only in this case, the customer operates a BPEL engine on his own an, therefore, could be in the situation to accept remotely defined BPEL scripts for execution on this engine. In the cases of PaaS and SaaS, the customer does not possess the BPEL engine, but only uses a BPEL engine provided to him (in PaaS) or uses an application that in turn, but without the conscious knowing of the customer, uses a BPEL engine (in SaaS). In PaaS, however, the customer could make use of the compliance assessment procedures described in Chapter 6 if an SPS is included in his SLA with the provider. In this case, the customer could assess the business processes for compliance to SLA prior to sending them to the provider for execution in order to avoid possible penalties by contract defined in the SLA for violation of SLA on the side of the customer.

The different aspects of transferability of the methods developed in the previous chapters for the different delivery models of Cloud computing are compiled in Table 9.

Table 9: Applicability of Methods from CBP Context to Cloud Delivery Models

Delivery Model	Point of View	Applicability
Infrastructure as a Service	Provider	Not relevant since provider does not operate BPEL engine
	Customer	Applicable since customer is in the same situation as in CBP context
Platform as a Service	Provider	Transferable as in Grid context. Provider can make SPS part of his SLA with his customers and assess compliance to SPS prior to execution each time a process is submitted for execution. If processes are encrypted for protection of customers assets contained, compliance assessment has to be amended to allow for decryption of the processes.
	Customer	Primarily, not applicable since customer does not operate BPEL engine. However, customer can assess compliance of BPEL script to SPS contained in SLA prior to submitting it for execution to the provider in order to avoid possible penalties by contract agreed upon with the provider.

Delivery Model	Point of View	Applicability
Software as a Service	Provider	Not applicable in the sense of CBP context because provider does not execute remotely defined BPEL scripts. However, security policy assessment procedures could be adopted for provider's quality assurance measures in developing new processes and adapting existing ones. The security policy to be enforced in this way would be the one of the provider, possibly amended by tenant-dependent aspects if tenant-specific processes are to be provided.
	Customer	Not applicable since customer does neither operate BPEL engine nor specify BPEL scripts for execution.

8.7 Summary

In this chapter, an approach to transfer the results achieved in the field of BPEL-defined business processes to other fields of application has been presented. Grid processes based on Grid services were chosen for this approach since BPEL is also used for the definition of the process logic in this context. In addition, Cloud environments also using BPEL for definition of processes or workflows have been considered in order to determine to which extent the results from the CBP area were also applicable to this field. Since the number of participants in a Grid process as well as the Grid services potentially invoked by such a process may be considerably higher than in a CBP context, the transfer of the results (though to a large extent possible with no or only minor modifications) may render difficult to handle because of the size and amount of SPSs involved. However, the transfer of the results from the CBP context is comparatively easy to be accomplished with respect to VOs, where the number of participants (or at least the number of roles involved) is in the same order of magnitude as with CBPs. Also the admission to become a member of a VO usually is regulated at least to a certain degree such that the members of a VO are comparatively constant over time and known in number. Therefore, VOs are comparable with the situation in CBPs and best suited for transfer of research results from the CBP context. Transfer of the results from the CBP context to other areas of Grid computing may be for further study.

In Cloud computing, the results were found to be applicable depending on the delivery model in place. Furthermore, distinction between the perspective of a provider of Cloud computing facilities and the one of a user of these facilities has turned out to be relevant. While with IaaS, the provider is not concerned with information flows in processes potentially executed on the hardware offered to his customers, a user running BPEL-enabled middleware on hardware provided as

IaaS is in nearly the same situation as if he were running the same middleware on hardware owned and operated by himself. With PaaS, the BPEL-enabled middleware could be offered by the provider as part of his service offering to his customers. Therefore, restrictions of access to certain Web services and avoidance of overload by service invocations known to be resource-intensive could be laid down in an SPS included in the SLA with customers. The observance of the restrictions in the SPS could be checked by the methods and procedures proposed here for CBPs and extended for Grid processes in this chapter. Conversely, the user of BPEL-enabled middleware provided as PaaS could also check the BPEL scripts to be run on this middleware prior to execution for compliance with the restrictions contain in his SLA with the provider. In this way, the user can avoid possible penalties by contract defined in the SLA in case the restrictions laid down in the SPS are violated by a process initiated by the user. With SaaS, there are no obvious applications of the methods and procedures presented here for a user. For a provider of BPEL-defined processes as SaaS, these methods may only be of interest in support of his quality assurance measures when developing new processes to be offered to his customers or when adapting existing ones to new or modified requirements.

Further research, in particular with respect to an alignment of insights with respect to security relevance of BPEL with results of research on Grid service semantics, may help to reduce the amount of information to be handled and may also prove successful in specifying restrictions indicated in an SPS at higher levels of abstraction.

9 Conclusions and Directions of Further Research and Development

To conclude and wrap up, this chapter summarises the achievements and limitations of the approaches presented in this book. It also considers possible directions of further research and development based on these results.

9.1 Which Contributions Have Been Achieved?

The increasing need for business-to-business applications has led to the specification of collaborative business processes (CBPs) using standardised specification languages. The de facto standard for this purpose is WS-BPEL (BPEL for short) that has been adopted as an OASIS standard in April 2007. Making full use of the fact that BPEL is a standard for specifying business processes, particularly executable ones, and, therefore, allows for definition of processes in a platform-independent way motivates the approach to specify a CBP at one location and have the different parts constituting this CBP executed on BPEL-enabled platforms of the respective partners involved in the CBP. Though technically feasible because BPEL-defined business processes are executable on any such platform, security issues involved in the execution of remotely defined business processes stand in the way of turning this approach into practical application. To mitigate or even eliminate these security issues, methods have been developed and presented in this book that allow for assessing the compliance of remotely defined business processes with local security policies prior to their execution. This assessment should preferably be performed automatically with as little as possible human intervention. At the same time, the assessment should incorporate methods for as fine-grained as possible an information flow control to avoid disadvantages of pure RBAC-based approaches that imply overly strict information flow control in order to securely avoid information leaks. Being able to have a remotely defined business process assessed for compliance with local security policies in an automatic way should allow for execution of the business process without security concerns.

In order to find methods that support compliance assessment in the manner aimed for, the security-relevant behaviour expressible in BPEL scripts has been investigated. The results of this investigation have been presented in Chapter 4. Based on an analysis and classification of security policy-induced restrictions to Web service invocation, combinations of restriction classes with BPEL activities called security-relevant semantic patterns have been analysed for their potential impact related to compliance with security policies. The derivation of these semantic patterns is depicted in Figure 24. Types of checks required for verification as to whether a BPEL script specifies behaviour that would violate security policies have also been indicated in Chapter 4.

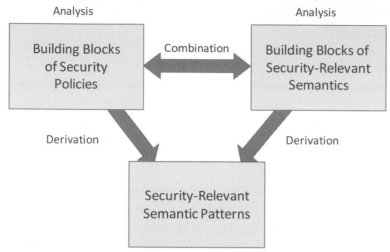

Figure 24: Approach to Definition of Security-Relevant Semantic Patterns

Based on the identification of security-relevant semantics of BPEL, a method for specifying security policies in such a way that the assessment of compliance with these policies is essentially facilitated has been introduced in Chapter 5. To this purpose, so-called security policy statements (SPSs) are used that indicate security policy-induced restrictions to Web services that are allowed to be invoked by a remotely defined business process. An approach to possibly reduce the complexity of an SPS is also introduced in this chapter, as well as an approach to cope with dynamic aspects of security policy-induced restrictions that by their very nature may only be checked at runtime of the process defined by a script.

The procedure of compliance assessment resulting from and enabled by these preparations have been described in Chapter 6. How a BPEL script under consideration is examined in order to assess its compliance with security policies as indicated in an SPS was described there. The novel approach to security policy enforcement enabled by the methods and procedures introduced in this book is outlined in Figure 25. After transformation of the relevant security policies into the formal representation introduced in Chapter 5, the compliance assessment reduces to searching business processes under consideration for occurrences of security-relevant semantic patterns that represent the restrictions implied by these security policies. This approach differs considerably from the approaches of related work as discussed in Chapter 3 and classified in Section 3.6 by the following aspects:

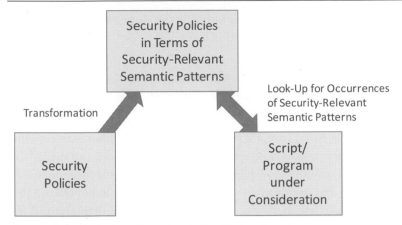

Figure 25: Approach to Security Policy Enforcement

- The compliance assessment to security policies is not performed at runtime, but is carried out prior to execution. Thereby, the weaknesses of approaches applied at runtime, in particular, the risk that violation of security policies might be detected too late to be prevented by appropriate intervention are avoided.

- The majority of approaches applicable prior to execution operate at an abstraction level above the actual programs or processes and the actual security policies. Therefore, they require both the security policies and the programs or processes to be checked in order to be transformed to a particular formalism or abstraction level in order to be able to perform compliance assessment as shown in Figure 6. The approach introduced here only requires security policies to be transformed while the BPEL scripts to be checked remain as they are during compliance assessment. Since security policies can be expected to be less susceptible to changes than business processes, the need for transformation to a formal representation is considerably less than with conventional approaches characterised by Figure 6. This may be considered an important advantage of this approach compared to these other approaches.

- The formalism into which security policies are to be transformed in order to be suited for compliance assessment with the new approach is based on representations that are common practice in the field of Web service and business process development, namely an XML-based representation of the restrictions derived from these security policies applicable to business processes. To go without any algebraic or other complex forms of representation as involved by most of the other approaches to security policy enforcement prior to execution discussed in Chapter 3 is another essential advantage of the approach introduced here. Practitioners in the field of Web service design and business process development who may have the need to check newly developed or modified business processes for compliance with security policies often are not acquainted with algebraic representations and how to work with them. To handle XML schemas and representations based thereon, however, can be considered daily business of practitioners in this field. Therefore, for them the new approach is supposed to be easy to apply.

Further in Chapter 6, the workflows involved if the assessment is performed in a distributed environment have been considered in order to discuss possibilities for delegation of the assessment procedure for economising the efforts required.

The viability of the methods for automatic performance of compliance assessment in the way proposed has been proved by implementing the essential parts of the assessment procedure in a prototype. Chapter 7 describes the machine-readable version of SPSs used and the architecture and algorithms implemented in this prototype. It further discusses the coverage of the total functionality required for automatic compliance assessment that has been achieved by this implementation. The discussion comes to the conclusion that the essential functionality of automatic compliance assessment has been implemented and that the missing parts are deducible in an easy manner from the functionality already realised or are straightforward to implement such that no templates are required to validate their feasibility. The evaluation performed led to the result that the methods proposed are suitable for automatic compliance assessment of BPEL scripts.

The novel methods for compliance assessment to security policies have been developed under the assumption that BPEL scripts as part of a CBP are defined by business process developers in one organisation being partner of the particular CBP and are brought to execution at the BPEL-enabled platform (BPEL engine and supporting equipment) of another organisation being another partner of the particular CBP. Though such distributed definition and execution scenarios across organisational boundaries seem not to be common practice to date, being able, prior to execution, to automatically assess compliance of BPEL-defined business processes to security policies of the executing site with hardly any human intervention underpins the validity and strength of this approach. Since these methods are suited to guarantee compliance to security policies under such conditions, they may be particularly appropriate to also support compliance assessment as part of quality assurance methods in purely local development of business processes (*i.e.*, BPEL scripts are defined and executed within the same organisation). Conventional approaches to compliance assessment prior to execution usually involve time-consuming procedures such as inspection techniques at code level (or script level in the case of BPEL). In particular, if adaptation to rapidly changing requirements matters, such conventional methods may pose problems with respect to timelines to be kept. It may be assumed that, in such situations, methods for automatic conformance assessment will be considered a welcome assistance and may be gladly adopted by the quality managers in charge to save time and effort.

To further complement the achievements reached so far, the approaches found have been transferred to other fields of application where similar conditions as with CBPs exist. The fields chosen are the area of Grid processes and the area of Cloud processes that can also be defined by BPEL scripts. The extent to which this transfer was successful within the given time scale of the project has been discussed in Chapter 8. Most of the results could be transferred in a straightforward manner to the area of Grid processing if virtual organisations (VOs) are considered and was found to be also applicable to certain areas in Cloud computing. However, new semantic patterns not considered in the context of CBPs had to be taken into account in the context of Grid and Cloud processing. In Cloud context, it turned out that the applicability or usefulness of the methods developed depends on the point of view of a customer or a provider of Cloud computing offerings. Also different Cloud delivery models such as IaaS, PaaS, or SaaS determine the applicability of the methods.

Obvious limitations mainly resulting from the larger amount of partners involved and of Grid/Web services eligible for invocation in a BPEL script defining a Grid/ Cloud process give rise to further research in this area. However, having shown that the results are transferable in principal to a related field of application may be considered to increase their significance.

Different aspects of the results presented here have been presented at refereed conferences or published in journals[191] and have received positive comments from delegates and reviewers.

9.2   What is Still to be Done?

Despite having met the objectives from the outset, some decisions had to be taken that resulted in limitations imposed on the work. The decisions were caused by practical reasons, or to limit the effort spent in areas where no new insights could be expected. These limitations are summarised below.

1. The prototype was restricted to only implement as much functionality of the assessment procedure as required to prove that the approach taken for facilitating compliance assessment was viable and that the methods developed were actually suited for automatic performance of this assessment. Therefore, the prototype does not cover all language features provided by the BPEL standard and, hence, is not suited to check arbitrary BPEL scripts for compliance with security policies. However, the XML schema provided for SPSs is complete in the sense that any security policy-induced restriction to Web service invocation as discussed in Chapter 4 may be specified. Implementing the missing parts to cover all of the BPEL capabilities was not expected to contribute new insights with respect to feasibility of an automatic compliance assessment procedure. Table 4 in Chapter 7.1, at least, contains directions how the missing parts could

---

191 Fischer *et al.*, 2005; Fischer *et al.*, 2006; Fischer *et al.*, 2007a; Fischer *et al.*, 2007b; Fischer *et al.*, 2007c; Fischer *et al.*, 2007d

be implemented in analogy to what already has been incorporated in the proto-type.

2. The algorithms used for covert channel detection in the prototype have been chosen to take a rigorous approach for effective prevention of any covert chan-nel from being established. However, these algorithms could turn out to be overly strict in some situations, for instance, if a branch is made dependent on visibility-restricted information and all alternative flows to be selected would not exhibit any distinguishable behaviour observable from outside. In such a situation, no covert channel would have been established by making the branch dependent on a visibility-restricted unit of information, but nevertheless a BPEL script containing this logic would have been refused by the prototypical com-pliance assessment procedure. Finding more sophisticated algorithms for covert channel detection that would be able to distinguish between actual covert channels and behaviour that only exhibits prima facie characteristics of a covert channel without actually establishing one have not deemed to be essential for a proof of concept. As already stated above, the definition of such algorithms that are both more tolerant with respect to covert channel detection and still secure in the sense that they do not leave any covert channel undetected may be difficult. Leaving decisions on doubtful behaviour possibly not suited to establish a covert channel to human intervention may also be a viable approach in cases where the rigorous approach for covert channel prevention implemen-ted in the prototype is found to be overly strict.

3. Similar to the previous item, restricting any inclusion of data manipulation faci-lities from other XML specifications such as XQuery, XSLT, or XPath in a BPEL script in order to be acceptable as compliant may also be deemed to be overly strict under certain circumstances. However, relaxation of this restriction with-out taking the risk to miss possible security policy violations during compliance assessment could also turn out to be a difficult task. In the same way as de-scribed for reduction of the complexity of security policy statements in Sec-tion 5.3, also any need for data manipulation in accordance with security policy that would require elements from XPath or other XML specifications to be in-cluded in a BPEL script can be moved into a Web service defined for that pur-pose. Therefore, this limitation is also not considered essential for the approach proposed.

4. Trying to integrate the prototypical implementation of a compliance assessment procedure into a BPEL-enabled platform though initially envisaged has been dropped. Reason for this was that access to such a platform for development purposes was not easy to obtain and this task would have required a tremen-dous amount of platform-specific know how to be acquired before the actual work would be possible. After all, this integration would by no means have contributed any particular insight or increased the confidence of viability. In effect, the proposed approach does not require that an automatic assessment

procedure is integrated into the platform where the BPEL script under consideration is intended to be executed once compliance assessment has been passed.
Quite the contrary, a stand-alone implementation of the assessment procedure
serves even better the intended goal to prevent a non-compliant BPEL script to
be executed since it even prevents such a script from entering the executing
platform at all.

5. During the course of the research and development the results of which have
   been presented herein, it became obvious that BPEL as the most prominent
   representative of a standardised business process definition language (BPDL)
   had emerged the de facto standard for defining executable business processes[192]. Since after completion of the development, BPMN has been argued by
   some authors to be better suited for business process definition than BPEL[193], an
   attempt to transfer the approaches proposed herein to other BPDLs could be the
   objective of further research. However, BPMN as a graphical notation apparently is not directly approachable by the methods developed here, which are based
   on XML notation of processes. Hence, conversion to an XML-based BPDL has to
   be performed prior to applying adapted versions of the methods for compliance
   assessment presented here. As XPDL seems to be the BPDL of choice for converting BPMN-defined processes into an XML representation, transferring the
   results achieved for BPEL to XPDL might be a worthwhile subject of further
   research and development.

Despite these limitations, the research and development that generated the results
presented in this book has led to valid contributions to knowledge and provided
sufficient proof of concept for the approaches proposed.

9.3 Directions of Further Research and Development

Though the results presented herein have advanced the field of security policy enforcement for script-based business processes, a number of areas for future work
can be identified that build upon the results achieved. Some ideas have already
been addressed in former chapters. These areas and some new ones are detailed
below.

1. Though already discussed as potentially difficult to find, the development of
   more sophisticated algorithms for covert channel detection in order to get rid of
   the rigorous yet effective approach taken in the prototype could be undertaken.
   The directions to be taken in an endeavour to relax this rigorous restriction have
   been indicated in the previous section. An outline of an algorithm for the relaxation of the restriction with respect to visibility-restricted information imposed

---

192 Pu *et al.*, 2006; Ouyang *et al.*, 2009
193 Vigneras, 2008; Swenson, 2008

to the `validate` activity and the attribute `validate` with a value of `true` in an `assign` activity can be found in Appendix 2.

2. Additional effort could be spent for completion of the prototypical implementation of the compliance assessment procedure. Though no new insights are expected to be gained thereof as argued above, having an implementation covering the whole of the capabilities provided by BPEL can be used for application to real world examples of BPEL scripts. This could assist in propagation of the ideas developed and presented here to a broader audience beyond academia.

3. In the attempt to transfer the results from the CBP context to the Grid and Cloud context, several issues for further research and development have been encountered. Amongst them the classification of (security-relevant) semantics of Grid and Web services and their parameters is deemed to be, at the same time, the most challenging and the most promising field for further study. Having such a classification of Grid/Web service semantics or characteristics thereof could advantageously be applied to reduce the amount of indications required in an SPS since enumeration of all Grid services or Web services accessible to Grid/Cloud processes, respectively, allowed for invocation in a BPEL script would no longer be required. In contrast, only the allowed Grid/ Web service semantics or characteristics would have to be indicated in an SPS. This approach would allow for compliance assessment of BPEL scripts invoking arbitrary Grid services or Web services, respectively, provided the semantics of the Grid/Web services or the characteristics derived thereof would also be specified in terms of the semantic classification scheme developed.

4. Investigating how the approaches proposed in Chapter 8 could be applied in practice based on Grid environments or Grid middleware such as The Globus Toolkit[194] or OurGrid[195] and Cloud service offerings such as Amazon Elastic Compute Cloud (Amazon EC2)[196] or Google's App Engine[197] and which adaptation would be required in order to be successful in doing this could be another interesting direction of further research and development.

---

194 http://www-unix.globus.org/toolkit
195 http://www.ourgrid.org
196 http://aws.amazon.com
197 http://appengine.google.com

Appendix 1: XML Schema for Security Policy Statement

This appendix contains an XML Schema specification for the security policy statement proforma (SPS) introduced in Chapter 5 that has been transferred into a
machine-processable XML-based form for the prototype as set out in Chapter 7.
The meaning of the elements and attributes defined in this schema has been
explained in Chapter 7. Therefore, they are not annotated in this schema definition.

```xml
<?xml version="1.0"?>
<xsd:schema
    xmlns:xsd="http://www.w3.org/2001/XMLSchema"
    xmlns="http://www.example.org/sps/SPS_Schema.xml"
    elementFormDefault="qualified"
    attributeFormDefault="unqualified"
    targetNamespace="http://www.example.org/sps/SPS_Schema.xml">
  <xsd:element name="sps">
    <xsd:complexType>
     <xsd:sequence>
       <xsd:element ref="identifications"/>
       <xsd:element ref="iwsrs" minOccurs="0"/>
       <xsd:element ref="ewsrs" minOccurs="0"/>
       <xsd:element ref="unrestrIntWs" minOccurs="0"/>
       <xsd:element ref="unrestrExtWs" minOccurs="0"/>
     </xsd:sequence>
    </xsd:complexType>
  </xsd:element>
<!-- +++++++++++++++++++++++++++++++++++++++++++++++++++ -->
<!-- +++++++++++++++ identifications ++++++++++++++++++ -->
<!-- +++++++++++++++++++++++++++++++++++++++++++++++++++ -->
  <xsd:element name="identifications">
   <xsd:complexType>
    <xsd:attribute name="remoteDomain" type="xsd:anyURI"
       use="required"/>
    <xsd:attribute name="localDomain" type="xsd:anyURI"
       use="required"/>
    <xsd:attribute name="applicationContext" type="xsd:anyURI"
       use="optional"/>
   </xsd:complexType>
  </xsd:element>
<!-- +++++++++++++++++++++++++++++++++++++++++++++++++++ -->
<!-- +++++++++++++++ restricted WS ++++++++++++++++++++ -->
<!-- +++++++++++++++++++++++++++++++++++++++++++++++++++ -->

<!-- +++++++++++++++++ external WS ++++++++++++++++++++ -->
  <xsd:element name="ewsrs">
   <xsd:complexType>
    <xsd:sequence>
     <xsd:element ref="operation" minOccurs="1"
       maxOccurs="unbounded"/>
    </xsd:sequence>
    <xsd:attribute name="internalUseAllowed" type="xsd:boolean"
```

```
                 use="optional" default="true"/>
      </xsd:complexType>
    </xsd:element>
!-- +++++++++++++++ internal WS +++++++++++++++++++ -->
    <xsd:element name="iwsrs"/>
      <xsd:complexType>
        <xsd:sequence>
          <xsd:element ref="operation" minOccurs="1"
             maxOccurs="unbounded"/>
        </xsd:sequence>
      </xsd:complexType>
    </xsd:element>
<!-- +++++++++++++++ operation +++++++++++++++++++++++ -->
    <xsd:element name="operation">
      <xsd:complexType>
        <xsd:sequence>
          <xsd:element ref="input"  minOccurs="0" maxOccurs="1"/>
          <xsd:element ref="output" minOccurs="0" maxOccurs="1"/>
        </xsd:sequence>
        <xsd:attribute name="name" type="xsd:string"
            use="required"/>
        <xsd:attribute name="portType" type="xsd:string"
            use="required"/>
      </xsd:complexType>
    </xsd:element>
<!-- +++++++++++++++++ input +++++++++++++++++++++++++ -->
    <xsd:element name="input">
      <xsd:complexType>
        <xsd:sequence>
          <xsd:element ref="sourceRestriction" minOccurs="0"
             maxOccurs="1"/>
          <xsd:element name="part" minOccurs="0"
             maxOccurs="unbounded">
          <xsd:complexType>
           <xsd:sequence>
            <xsd:element ref="sourceRestriction" minOccurs="0"/>
            <xsd:element ref="valueRestriction"  minOccurs="0"/>
           </xsd:sequence>
           <xsd:attribute name="name" type="xsd:string"
                 use="required"/>
           <xsd:attribute name="sourceRestricted"
                 type="xsd:boolean" use="optional" default="false"/>
           <xsd:attribute name="valueRestricted"
                 type="xsd:boolean" use="optional" default="false"/>
           <xsd:attribute name="restrictedOptional"
                 use="optional"    default="presentOrNot">
            <xsd:simpleType>
              <xsd:restriction base="xsd:string">
               <xsd:enumeration value="presentOrNot"/>
               <xsd:enumeration value="forbiddenPart"/>
               <xsd:enumeration value="requiredPart"/>
              </xsd:restriction>
            </xsd:simpleType>
           </xsd:attribute>
          </xsd:complexType>
        </xsd:sequence>
```

```xml
        <xsd:attribute name="message" type="xsd:string"/>
        <xsd:attribute name="sourceRestricted"
            type="xsd:boolean"
            use="optional" default="false"/>
    </xsd:complexType>
</xsd:element>

<xsd:element name="sourceRestriction">
  <xsd:complexType>
    <xsd:sequence>
      <xsd:element ref="service"
          minOccurs="1" maxOccurs="unbounded"/>
    </xsd:sequence>
  </xsd:complexType>
</xsd:element>

<xsd:element name="valueRestriction">
  <xsd:complexType>
    <xsd:sequence>
      <xsd:element name="permittedValue" type="anyType"
          minOccurs="1" maxOccurs="unbounded"/>
    </xsd:sequence>
  </xsd:complexType>
</xsd:element>

<xsd:element name="service">
  <xsd:complexType>
    <xsd:attribute name="portType" type="xsd:string"/>
    <xsd:attribute name="operation" type="xsd:string"/>
  </xsd:complexType>
</xsd:element>

<!-- +++++++++++++++++++ output +++++++++++++++++++++ -->
<xsd:element name="output">
  <xsd:complexType>
    <xsd:sequence>
      <xsd:element ref="targetRelaxation" minOccurs="0"/>
      <xsd:element name="part"
          minOccurs="0" maxOccurs="unbounded">
        <xsd:complexType>
          <xsd:sequence>
            <xsd:element ref="targetRelaxation" minOccurs="0"/>
          </xsd:sequence>
          <xsd:attribute name="name" type="xsd:string"
              use="required"/>
          <xsd:attribute name="visibilityRestricted"
              type="xsd:boolean" use="optional" default="true"/>
        </xsd:complexType>
      </xsd:element>
    </xsd:sequence>
    <xsd:attribute name="message" type="xsd:string"/>
    <xsd:attribute name="visibilityRestricted"
        type="xsd:boolean" use="optional" default="false"/>
  </xsd:complexType>
</xsd:element>
```

```xml
  <xsd:element name="targetRelaxation">
   <xsd:complexType>
    <xsd:sequence>
     <xsd:element name="domain" type="xsd:anyURI"
        minOccurs="1" maxOccurs="unbounded"/>
    </xsd:sequence>
   </xsd:complexType>
  </xsd:element>


<!-- ++++++++++++++++++++++++++++++++++++++++++++++++++++ -->
<!-- +++++++++++++++++ unrestricted WS +++++++++++++++++ -->
<!-- ++++++++++++++++++++++++++++++++++++++++++++++++++++ -->

  <xsd:element name="unrestrExtWs">
   <xsd:complexType>
    <xsd:sequence>
     <xsd:element name="operation"
        minoccurs="1" maxOccurs="unbounded">
      <xsd:complexType>
       <xsd:attribute name="name" type="xsd:string"
            use="required"/>
       <xsd:attribute name="portType" type="xsd:string"
            use="required"/>
      </xsd:complexType>
     </xsd:element>
    </xsd:sequence>
   </xsd:complexType>
  </xsd:element>

  <xsd:element name="unrestrIntWs">
   <xsd:sequence>
    <xsd:element name="operation" minoccurs="1"
        maxOccurs="unbounded">
     <xsd:complexType>
      <xsd:attribute name="name" type="xsd:string"
          use="required"/>
      <xsd:attribute name="portType" type="xsd:string"
          use="required"/>
     </xsd:complexType>
    </xsd:element>
   </xsd:sequence>
  </xsd:element>

</xsd:schema>
```

Appendix 2: Outline of Sophisticated Covert Channel Prevention for Activity `validate`

In order to allow for type validation of a variable containing visibility-restricted information in cases where no risk of information leakage exists, it has to be made sure that throwing the standard `bpel:invalidVariables` fault does not allow conclusions to be drawn as to the value of the information currently contained in this variable. Validation with respect to the proper type of the value contained in a variable may either be caused by a `validate` activity or by indication of attribute `validate="true"` in an `assign` activity. A more sophisticated check for covert channel prevention with type validation than that proposed in the main part of the book would require assuring that no value restricted subtype of a type is being applied in validation.

Therefore, the more sophisticated check for covert channel detection with type validation would allow a variable containing visibility-restricted information to be validated provided its type definition does not imply any restrictions with respect to the value of this variable. This can be checked by inspection of the message type in a WSDL definition or the type definition in an XML schema containing the type definition for the variable under consideration. The XML type definition found for the particular variable must neither contain any `<restriction>` element nor must the type be defined by a `<list>` element nor by a `<union>` element containing any type definition constrained by any of the aforementioned elements.

If the type can be verified in this way to not implying any value range restrictions for the variable under consideration, then type validation may be allowed even in the case where the variable currently contains a value that represents visibility-restricted information.

References

Aalst, W. M. P. v. d., Dumas, M., ter Hofsted, A. H. M., and Wohed, P. (2002) "Pattern Based Analysis of BPML (and WSCI)". Technical Report FIT-TR-2002-05, Queensland University of Technology, 2002, http://citeseerx.ist.psu.edu/viewdoc/download?doi=10.1.1.11.7424&rep=rep1&type=pdf, last accessed 2012-01-20.

Aalst, W. M. P. v. d., Weijters, T., and Maruster, L. (2004) "Workflow mining: Discovering process models from event logs". *IEEE Transactions on Knowledge and Data Engineering*, 16(9):1128–1142.

Abendroth, J. and Jensen, C. D. (2003) "Partial Outsourcing: A New Paradigm for Access Control". In *Proc. 8th ACM Symposium on Access Control Models and Technologies, (SACMAT'03)*, pp. 134–141.

Abou El Kalam, A., El Baida, R., Balbiani, P., Benferhat, S., Cuppens, F., Deswarte, Y., Miège, A.,Saurel, C., and Troussin, G. (2003) "Organization Based Access Control". In *Proc 4th IEEE International Workshop on Policies for Distributed Systems and Networks (Policy'03)*, pp. 120–134.

Accorsi, R. and Wonnemann, C. (2010) "InDico: information flow analysis of business processes for confidentiality requirements". In *Proc. 6th international conference on Security and trust management (STM'10)*, pp. 194–209.

Accorsi, R. and Wonnemann, C. (2011) "Strong non-leak guarantees for workflow models". In *Proc. 2011 ACM Symposium on Applied Computing (SAC '11)*, pp. 308–314.

Agrawal, R., Gunopulos, D., and Leymann, F. (1998) "Mining process models from workflow logs". In *Proc. 6th International Conference on Extending Database Technology*, pp. 469–483.

Aymerich, F., Fenu, G., and Surcis, S. (2008) "An approach to a cloud computing network", in *Proc. 1st International Conference on the Applications of Digital Information and Web Technologies (ICADIWT 2008)*, pp. 113–118.

Alves, A., Arkin, A., Askary, S., Barreto, C., Bloch, B., Curbera, F., Ford, M., Goland, Y., Guizar, A., Kartha, N., Liu, C. K., Khalaf, R., König, D., Marin, M., Mehta, V., Thatte, S., van der Rijn, D., Yendluri, P., and Yiu, A., eds. (2007) "Web Services Business Process Execution Language Version 2.0". OASIS, http://docs.oasis-open.org/wsbpel/2.0/OS/wsbpel-v2.0-OS.pdf, last accessed 2012-01-20.

Amnuaykanjanasin, P. and Nupairoj, N. (2005) "The BPEL Orchestrating Framework for Secured Grid Services", In *Proc. International Conference on Information Technology: Coding and Computing (ITCC'05)*, Vol. I, pp. 348–353.

Anstett, T., Leymann, F., Mietzner, R., and Strauch, S. (2009) "Towards BPEL in the Cloud: Exploiting Different Delivery Models for the Execution of Business Processes". In *Proc. International Workshop on Cloud Services (IWCS 2009)*, pp. 670–677.

Arkin, A. (2002) "Business Process Modeling Language". BPMI.org, http://xml. coverpages.org/BPML-2002.pdf, last accessed 2012-01-20.

Arkin, A., Askary, S., Bloch, B., Curbera, F. Goland, Y., Kartha, N., Liu, C. K., Thatte, S., and Yendluri, eds. (2004) "Web Services Business Process Execution Language Version 2.0". Working Draft, OASIS, http://www.oasis-open.org/apps/workgroup/ wsbpel, last access: 2012-01-20.

Arkin, A., Askary, S., Fordin, S., Jekeli, W., Kawaguchi, K., Orchard, D., Pogliani, S., Riemer, K., Struble, S., Takacsi-Nagy, P., Trickovic, I., and Zimek, S., eds. (2002) "Web Service Choreography Interface (WSCI) 1.0". World Wide Web Consortium, http://www.w3.org/TR/2002/NOTE-wsci-20020808, last accessed 2012-01-20.

Bacon, J., Moody, K., and Yao, W. (2002) "A Model of OASIS Role-Based Access Control and Its Support for Active Security". *ACM Trans. Information and System Security*, 5(4):492–540.

Bajaj, S., Box, B., Chappell, D., Curbera, F., Daniels, G., Hallam-Baker, P., Hondo, M., Kaler, C., Langworthy, D., Nadalin, A., Nagaratnam, N., Prafullchandra, H., von Riegen, C., Roth, D., Schlimmer, J., Sharp, C., Shewchuk, J., Vedamuthu, A., Yalçinalp, Ü., and Orchard, D. (2006) "Web Services Policy 1.2 – Framework (WS-Policy)". World Wide Web Consortium, http://www.w3.org/Submission/2006/SUBM-WS-Policy-20060425, last accessed 2012-01-20.

Barbuti, R., Bernardeschi, C., and De Francesco, N. (2002) "Checking Security of Java Bytecode by Abstract Interpretation". In *Proc. 17th ACM Symposium on Applied Computing (SAC'2002)*, pp. 229–236.

Beco S., Cantalupo B., Giammarino L., Matskanis N., and Surridge, M. (2005) "OWL-WS: A Workflow Ontology for Dynamic Grid Service Composition", In *Proc. 1st International Conference on e-Science and Grid Computing (E-SCIENCE '05)*, pp. 148–155.

Berardi, D., De Rosa, F., De Santis, L., and Mecella, M. (2003) "Finite State Automata as Conceptual Model for E-Services". In *Proc. 7th World Conference on Integrated Design and Process Technology, IDPT-2003*.

Berglund, A., Boag, S., Chamberlin, D., Fernández, M. F., Kay, M., Robie, J., and Siméon, J., eds. (2006) "XML Path Language (XPath) 2.0". World Wide Web Consortium, 2006, http://www.w3.org/ TR/xpath20, last accessed 2012-01-20.

Biron, P. V. and Malhotra, A., eds. (2004) "XML Schema Part 2: Datatypes Second Edition". World Wide Web Consortium, http://www.w3.org/TR/2004/REC-xml schema-2-20041028, last accessed: 2012-01-20.

Boag, S., Chamberlin, D., Fernández, M. F., Florescu, D., Robie, J., and Siméon, J., eds. (2007) "XQuery 1.0: An XML Query Language (Second Edition)" W3C Recommendation, World Wide Web Consortium, http://www.w3.org/TR/xquery, last accessed: 2012-01-23.

Botha, R. A. and Eloff, J. H. O. (2001) "Separation of duties for access control enforcement in workflow environments". *IBM System Journal*, 40 (3), 666–682, 2001.

Box, D., Ehnebuske, D., Kakivaya, G., Layman, A., Mendelsohn, N., Nielsen, H. F., Thatte, S., and Winer, D., eds. (2000) "Simple Object Access Protocol (SOAP) 1.1" World Wide Web Consortium, http://www.w3.org/TR/2000/NOTE-SOAP-20000508, last accessed: 2012-01-20.

Bray, T., Paoli, J., Sperberg, C. M., Maler, E., and Yergeau, F., eds. (2006) "Extensible Markup Language (XML) 1.0 (Fourth Edition)". World Wide Web Consortium, http://www.w3.org/TR/2006/REC-xml-20060816, last accessed: 2012-01-20.

BSI (2009) "SOA-Security-Kompendium - Sicherheit in Service-orientierten Architekturen, Version 2.0", Bundesamt für Sicherheit in der Informationstechnik (BSI), Bonn, Germany, https://www.bsi.bund.de/SharedDocs/Downloads/DE/BSI/SOA/SOA-Security-Kompendium_pdf.pdf?_blob=publicationFile,last accessed:2011-12-29

Bustamente, M. L. (2007) "Making Sense of all these Crazy Web Service Standards". InfoQ.com, http://www.infoq.com/articles/ws-standards-wcf-bustamente, last accessed: 2012-01-20.

Cantor, S., Kemp, J., Philpott, R., and Maler, E. (2005) "Assertions and Protocols for the OASIS Security Assertion Language (SAML) V2.0". OASIS, http://docs.oasis-open.org/security/saml/v2.0/saml-core-2.0-os.pdf, last accessed 2012-01-20.

Chadwick D. W., Su, L., and Laborde, R. (2006) "Providing Secure Coordinated Access to Grid Services",: In *Proc. 4th International Workshop on Middleware for Grid Computing (MCG '06)*, pp. 1–6.

Chinnici, R., Moreau, J. J., Ryman, A., and Weerawarana, S., eds. (2007) "Web Services Description Language (WSDL) 2.0 Part 1: Core Language". World Wide Web Consortium, http://www.w3.org/TR/wsdl20, last accessed 2012-01-20.

Christensen, E., Curbera, F. , Meredith, G., and Weerawarana, S. (2001) "Web Services Description Language (WSDL) 1.1". World Wide Web Consortium, http://www.w3.org/TR/2001/NOTE-wsdl-20010315, last accessed 2012-01-20.

Chong, S. and Myers, A.C. (2004) "Security Policies for Downgrading". In *Proc. 11th ACM Conference on Computer and Communications Security (CCS'04)*, pp. 198–209.

Clement, L., Hately, A., von Riegen, C., and Rogers, T. (2004) "UDDI Version 3.0.2". OASIS, http://uddi.org/pubs/uddi_v3.htm, last accessed: 2012-01-20.

Coetzee, M. and Eloff, J. H. P. (2003) "Virtual Enterprise Access Control Requirements". In Proc. 2003 annual research conference of the South African institute of computer scientists and information technologists on Enablement through technology, pp. 285–294.

Cousot, P. (1999) "Directions for research in approximate system analysis". *ACM Computing Surveys (CSUR)*, 31(3es), 5 pages.

Curbera, F., Khalaf, R., Mukhi, N., Tai, S., and Weerawarana, S. (2003) "The Next Step in Web Services". *Communications of the ACM*, 46(10):29–34.

Deng, W., Yang, X., Zhao, H., Dan, L., and Li, H. (2008) "Study on EAI Based on Web Services and SOA". In *Proc. 2008 International Symposium on Electronic Commerce and Security (ISECS '08)*, pp. 95–98.

Detsch, A., Gaspary, L. P., Barcellos, M. P., and Cavalheiro, G. G. H. (2004) "Towards a Flexible Security Framework for Peer-to-Peer-based Grid Computing". In *Proc. 2nd Workshop on Middleware for Grid Computing (MGC'04)*, pp. 52–56.

Deubler, M., Grünbauer, J., Jürjens, J., and Wimmel, G. (2004) "Sound Development of Secure Service-based Systems", In *Proc. 2nd International Conference on Service Oriented Computing, (ICSOC'04)*, pp. 115-124.

Dickson, K. W. C., Cheung, S. C., Till, S., Karlapalem, K., Li, Q., and Kafeza, E. (2004) "Workflow View Driven Cross-Organisational Interoperability in Web Service Environment" *Information Technology and Management*, 5:221–250, Kluwer Academic Publishers.

Dimmock, N., Belokosztolszki, A., Eyers, D., Bacon, J., and Moody, K. (2004) "Using Trust and Risk in Role-Based Access Control Policies". In *Proc. 9th ACM Symposium on Access Control Models and Technologies (SACMAT'04)*, pp. 156–162.

Dobson, J. (1994) "Messages, Communications, Information Security and Value". In Proc. *1994 workshop on New security paradigms*, pp. 10–19.

Dubray, J. J., Amand, S. St., Martin, M. J. (2006) "ebXML Business Process Specification Schema, Version 2.0.4". OASIS,. http://docs.oasis-open.org/ebxml-bp/2.0.4/ebxmlbp-v2.0.4-Spec-os-en.pdf, last accessed 2020-01-20.

Echahed, R. and Prost. F. (2005) "Security Policy in a Declarative Style". In *Proc. 7th ACM SIGPLAN International Conference on Principles and Practice of Declarative Programming, PPDP'05*, pp. 153–163.

Esfahani, F. S., Murad, M. A. A., Sulaiman, M. N. B., and Udzir, N. I. (2011) "Adaptable Decentralized Service Oriented Architecture". *J. Syst. Softw.*, 84(10), pp. 1591–1617.

Ferraiolo, D. F. and Kuhn, D. R. (1992) "Role-Based Access Control". In *Proc. 15th National Computer Security Conference*, pp. 554–563.

Ferraiolo, D., Cugini, J., and Kuhn, R. (1995) "Role Based Access Control (RBAC): Features and Motivations". In *Proc. 11th Annual Computer Security Applications Conference*, pp. 241-248.

Ferraiolo, D., Sandhu, R., Gavrila, S., Kuhn, R., Chandramouli, R. (2001) "Proposed NIST standard for role-based access control". *ACM Trans. Information and System Security (TISSEC)*, 4(3):224-274.

Fielding, R., Gettys, J., Mogul, J., Frystyk, H., Masinter, L., Leach, P., and Berners-Lee., T. (1999) "Hypertext Transfer Protocol – HTTP/1.1". RFC 2616. IETF, http://www.ietf.org/rfc/rfc2616.txt, last accessed 2012-01-20.

Fischer, K. P., Bleimann, U., Fuhrmann, W., and Furnell, S. M. (2005) "A Security Infrastructure for Cross-Domain Deployment of Script-Based Business Processes in

SOC Environments". In *Proc. 5th International Network Conference, INC'2005*, pp. 207–216.

Fischer, K. P., Bleimann, U., Fuhrmann, W., and Furnell, S. M. (2006) "Security-Relevant Semantic Patterns of BPEL in Cross-Organisational Business Processes". In *Proc. 6th International Network Conference, INC'2006*, pp. 203–212.

Fischer, K. P., Bleimann, U., Fuhrmann, W., and Furnell, S. M. (2007a) "Security Policy Enforcement in BPEL-Defined Collaborative Business Processes". In *Proc. 1st International Workshop on Security Technologies for Next Generation Collaborative Business Applications (SECOBAP'07)*, IEEE Computer Society, pp. 685–694.

Fischer, K. P., Bleimann, U., Fuhrmann, W., and Furnell, S. M. (2007b) "Analysis of Security-Relevant Semantics of BPEL in Cross-Domain Defined Business Processes". *Information Management & Computer Security*, 15(2):116–127.

Fischer, K. P., Bleimann, U., Fuhrmann, W., and Furnell, S. M. (2007c) "Security-Relevance of Semantic Patterns in Cross-Organisational Business Processes Using WS-BPEL". In *Proc. 3rd Collaborative Research Symposium on Security, E-learning, Internet and Networking (SEIN 2007)*, University of Plymouth, pp. 67–83.

Fischer, K. P., Bleimann, U., and Furnell, S. M. (2007d) „Pre-Execution Security Policy Assessment of Remotely Defined BPEL-Based Grid Processes". In *Proc. 4th International Conference on Trust, Privacy & Security in Digital Business (TrustBus'07)*, Springer, LNCS 4657, pp. 178–189.

Fischer, O. and Wenzel, B. (2004) "Prozessorientierte Dienstleistungsunterstützung: Workflowbasierte Komposition unternehmensübergreifender Geschäftsprozesse", University of Hamburg, http://vsis-www.informatik.uni-hamburg.de/publications/viewThesis.php/177, last accessed: 2012-01-20.

Foster, I., Kesselman, C., Nick, J., and Tuecke, S. (2002) "The Physiology of the Grid: An Open Grid Services Architecture for Distributed Systems Integration, Globus Project, http://www.globus.org/alliance/publications/papers/ogsa.pdf, last accessed: 2012-01-20.

Foster, I., Kesselman, C., and Tuecke, S. (2001) "The Anatomy of the Grid: Enabling Scalable Virtual Organizations", *Int. J. High Perform. Comput. Appl.*, 15(3):200–222.

Foster, I. and Tuecke, S. (2005) "Describing the Elephant: The Different Faces of IT as Service". *Enterprise Distributed Computing, Queue*, 3(6):27–34.

Fundulaki, I. and Marx, M. (2004) "Specifying Access Control Policies for XML Documents with Xpath". In *Proc. 9th ACM Symposium on Access Control Models and Technologies, (SACMAT'04)*, pp. 61–69.

Gannon, D., Krishnan, S., Fang, L., Kandaswamy, G., Simmhan, Y., and Slominsk, A. (2005) "On Building Parallel & Grid Applications: Component Technology and Distributed Services". *Cluster Computing*, 8(4):271–277, Kluwer Academic Publishers.

Goble, C. and De Roure, D. (2002) "The Grid: An Application of the Semantic Web", *SIGMOD Rec.*, 31(4):65–70.

Godik, S. and Moses, T., eds. (2003) "eXtensible Access Control Markup Language (XACML) Version 1.0", OASIS, http://www.oasis-open.org/committees/download.php/2406/oasis-xacml-1.0.pdf, last accessed: 2012-01-20.

Goguen, J. A. and Meseguer, J. (1982) "Security policies and security models". In *Proc. IEEE Symposium. on Security and Privacy*, pp. 11–20.

Haller, A. and Oren, E. (2006) "A Process Ontology to Represent Semantics of Different Process and Choreography Meta-Models". DERI Technical Report 2006-02-03, Digital Enterprise Research Institute, http://www.armin-haller.com/publications/DERI-TR-2006-02-03.pdf, last accessed: 2012-01-20.

Haller, A., Oren, E., and Kotinurmi, P. (2006) "An Ontology for Internal and External Business Processes". In *Proc. 15th International World Wide Web Conference (WWW'06)*, pp. 1055–1056.

Hao, T., Hu, D., Wenyin, L., and Zeng, Q. (2008) "Semantic patterns for user-interactive question answering". *Concurrency Computat.: Pract. Exper.* 20(7):783–799.

Hitachi (2006) "Beyond Roles: A Practical Approach to Enterprise User Provisioning". White Paper, Hitachi ID Systems, Inc., Calgary, Canada, 2006, http://hitachi-id.com/identity-manager/docs/beyond-roles.pdf, last accessed: 2012-01-30.

Höing, A. (2010) "Orchestrating Secure Workflows for Cloud and Grid Services". PhD Thesis, Technical University Berlin, Faculty IV.

Hummer, W., Gaubatz, P., Strembeck, M., Zdun, U., and Dustdar, S. (2011) "An integrated approach for identity and access management in a SOA context". In *Proc. 16th ACM symposium on Access control models and technologies (SACMAT '11)*, pp. 21–30.

Iyengar, A., Jessani, V., and Chilanti,M. (2007) "WebSphere Business Integration Primer: Process Server, Bpel, Sca, and SOA (1st ed.)". IBM Press.

ISO (1994) "ISO/IEC 9646-5:1994 Information technology – Open Systems Interconnection – Conformance testing methodology and framework – Part 5: Requirements on test laboratories and clients for the conformance assessment process". International Organisation for Standardization, Geneve.

ITU/UN (2007) "Challenges to building a safe and secure Information Society". In *World Information Society Report 2007*, International Telecommunication Union and United Nations, http://www.itu.int/osg/spu/publications/worldinformationsociety/2007/WISR07full-free.pdf, last accessed: 2012-01-20.

Jellema, L. and Dikmans, L. (2010) "Oracle SOA Suite 11g Handbook (1st ed.)". McGraw-Hill, Inc., New York.

Joshi, J. B. D., Aref, W. G., Ghafoor, A., and Spafford, E. H. (2001) "Security Models for Web-Based Applications". *Communications of the ACM*, 44(2):38–44.

Kay, M., ed. (2007) "XSL Transformations (XSLT) Version 2.0" W3C Recommendation, World Wide Web Consortium, http://www.w3.org/TRxslt20/, last accessed: 2012-01-23.

Knorr, K. (2001) "Multilevel Security and Information Flow in Petri Net Work-flows". In *Proc. 11th Conference on Advanced Information Systems Engineering*, pp. 9–20.

Koshutanski, H. and Massacci, F. (2003) "An Access Control Framework for Business Processes for Web Services". In *Proc. 2003 ACM Workshop on XML Security*, pp. 15–24.

Kuper, G., Massacci, F., and Rassadko, N. (2005) "Generalized XML Security Views". In *Proc. 10th Symposium on Access Control Models and Technologies (SACMAT'05)*, pp. 77–84.

Lampson, B. W. (1973) "A note on the confinement problem". *Communications of the ACM*, 16(10):613–615.

Leymann, F. (2001) "Web Service Flow Language (WSFL 1.0)". IBM, 2001, http://xml.coverpages.org/WSFL-Guide-200110.pdf, last accessed: 2012-01-20.

Leymann, F. and Roller, D. (2004) "Modelling Business Process with BPEL4WS". In *Proc. 1st Workshop on XML Interchange Formats for Business Process Management (XML4BPM'2004)*, pp. 7–24.

Li, P. and Zdancewic, S. (2005) "Downgrading Policies and Relaxed Noninterference". In *Proc. 32nd ACM Symposium on Principles of Programming Languages (POPL'05)*, pp. 158–170.

Lippe, S., Greiner, U., and Barros A. (2005) "Survey on State of the Art to Facilitate Modelling of Cross-Organisational Business Processes". In *Proc. 2nd Workshop on XML Interchange Formats for Business Process Management (XML4BPM'2005)*, pp. 7–22, http: //citeseerx.ist.psu.edu/viewdoc/download;jsessionid=6B60A313F9B8BA 9E699FC9C085FFADA?doi=10.1.1.59.1974&rep=rep1&type=pdf, last accessed: 2012-01-20.

Lorch, M., Proctor, S., Lepro, R., Kafura, D., and Shah, S. (2003) "First Experiences Using XACML for Access Control in Distributed Systems". In *Proc. 2003 ACM Workshop on XML Security*, pp. 25–37.

Ludwig S. A., and Reyhani, S. M. S. (2005) "Introduction of Semantic Matchmaking to Grid Computing", *J. Parallel Distrib. Comput.*, 65(12):1533–1541.

MacKenzie, C., Laskey, K., McCabe, F., Brown, P. F., and Metz, R. eds. (2006) "Reference Model for Service Oriented Architecture 1.0". OASIS Standard, http://docs.oasis-open.org/soa-rm/v1.0/soa-rm.pdf, last accessed: 2012-01-28.

Mayer, P. and Lübke, D. (2006) "Towards a BPEL unit testing framework". In *Proc. 2006 Workshop on Testing, Analysis, and Verification of Web Services and Applications*, pp. 33–42.

Medjahed, B., Benatallah, B., Bouguettayaet, A., Ngu, A. H. H., and Elmagarmid, A. K. (2003) "Business-to-business interactions: issues and enabling technologies". *VLDB Journal (2003)* 12:59–85.

Mendling, J., Strembeck, M., Sternsek, G., and Neumann, G. (2004) "An Approach to Extract RBAC Models from BPEL4WS Processes". In *Proc. 13th IEEE International*

Workshops on Enabling Technologies: Infrastructures for Collaborative Enterprises (WET ICE 2004), pp. 81–86.

Merouani, H., Mokhati, F., and Seridi-Bouchelaghem, H. (2010) "Towards formalizing web service composition in Maude's strategy language". In *Proc. 1st International Conference on Intelligent Semantic Web-Services and Applications (ISWSA '10)*, Article 15 , 6 pages.

Miller, J. A., Fan, M., Sheth, A., and Kochut, K. J. (1997) "Security in Web-Based Workflow Management Systems". Technical Report, University of Georgia.

Moses, T., ed. (2005) "eXtensible Access Control Markup Language (XACML) Version 2.0", OASIS, http://docs.oasis-open.org/xacml/2.0/access_control-xacml-2.0-core-spec-os.pdf, last accessed: 2012-01-20.

Nadalin, A., Goodner, M., Barbir, A., and Granqvist, H., eds. (2007a) "WS-Security Policy 1.2", OASIS, http://docs.oasis-open.org/ws-sx/ws-securitypolicy/200702/ws-securitypolicy-1.2-spec-os.html, last accessed: 2012-01-20.

Nadalin, A., Goodner, M., Gudgin, M., Barbir, A., and Granqvist, H., eds. (2007b) "WS-Trust 1.3", OASIS, http://docs.oasis-open.org/ws-sx/ws-trust/200512/ws-trust-1.3-os.html, last accessed: 2012-01-20.

Nadalin, A., Kahler, C., Monzillo, R., and Hallam-Baker, P., eds. (2006) "Web Services Security: SOAP Message Security 1.1 (WS-Security 2004)". OASIS, http://www.oasis-open.org/committees/download.php/16790/wss-v1.1-spec-os-SOAPMessageSecurity.pdf, last accessed: 2012-01-20.

Necula, G. (1997) "Proof Carrying Code". In *Proc 24th ACM Symposium on Principles of Programming Languages*, pp. 106–119.

Nordio, M.; Bavera, F.; Medel, R.; Aguirre, J.; Baum, G. (2004) "A Framework for Execution of Secure Mobile Code based on Static Analysis". In *Proc. 24th International Conference of the Chilean Computer Science Society (SCCC 2004)*, pp. 59–66.

OASIS (2007) "Members Approve Web Service Business Process Execution Language (WS-BPEL) as OASIS Standard". http://www.oasis-open.org/news/ws-bpel-press-release.pdf, last accessed: 2012-01-20.

The Open Group (2011) "SOA Reference Architecture". Technical Standard, The Open Group, http://www.opengroup.org/projects/soa-ref-arch, last accessed: 2012-01-28.

OMG (2011) "Business Process Model and Notation (BPMN), Version 2.0", OMG standard, http://www.omg.org/spec/BPMN/2.0, last accessed: 2012-01-29.

Ouyang, C., Dumas, M., Van Der Aalst, W. M. P., Ter Hofstede, A. H. M., and Mendling, J. (2009) "From business process models to process-oriented software systems". *ACM Trans. Softw. Eng. Methodol.*, 19(1), Article 2, 37 pages.

Papazoglou, M. P. and Georgakopoulos, D. (2003) "Service-Oriented Computing". *Communications of ACM*, 46(10):25–28.

Papazoglou, M. P. and van den Heuvel, W.-J., (2007) "Service oriented architectures: approaches, technologies and research issues". *VLDB Journal*, 16:389–415.

Peng, L. and Chen, Z. (2004) "An Access Control Model for Web Services in Business Process". In *Proc. IEEE/WIC/ACM International Conference on Web Intelligence (WI'04)*, pp. 292–298.

Pu, G., Zhao, X., Wang, S., and Qiu, Z. (2006) "Towards the Semantics and Verification of BPEL4WS". *Electron. Notes Theor. Comput. Sci.*, 151(2):33–52.

Ren, K., Xiao, N., Song, J., Chen, T., and Zhang, W. (2006) "A Model for Semantic Annotation and Publication of Meteorology Grid Services in SMGA", In *Proc. 5th International Conference on Grid and Cooperative Computing Workshops (GCCW'06)*, pp. 496–503.

Ribeiro, C., Zúquete, A., Ferreira, P., and Guedes, P. (2000) "Security policy consistency". In *Proc. Workshop on Rule-Based Constraint Reasoning and Programming*.

Ribeiro, C., Zúquete, A., Ferreira, P., and Guedes, P. (2001) "SPL: An access control language for security policies with complex constraints". In *Proc. Network and Distributed System Security Symposium (NDSS'01)*, pp. 1–12.

Rubin, A. D. and Geer, D. E., Jr. (1998) "Mobile Code Security". *Internet Computing*, 2(6):30–34.

Roser, S., Müller, J. P., and Bauer, B. (2011) "An evaluation and decision method for ICT architectures for cross-organizational business process coordination". *Inf. Syst. E-bus. Manag.*, 9(1):51–88.

Sabelfeld, A., Myers, A. C. (2003) "Language-Based Information-Flow Security". *IEEE Journal on Selected Areas in Communications*, 21(1):5–19.

Sayaha J. Y. and Zhang, L.-J. (2005) "On-demand business collaboration enablement with web services". *Decision Support Systems*, 40:107–127, Elsevier.

Schaad., A. and Moffett, J. J. (2002) "A Lightweight Approach to Specification and Analysis of Role-based Access Control Extensions". In *Proc. 7th ACM Symposium on Access Control Models and Technologies (SACMAT'06)*, pp. 13–22.

Schaad, A., Lotz, V., Sohr, K. (2006) „A Model-checking Approach to Analysing Organisational Controls in a Loan Origination Process". In *Proc. 11th ACM Symposium on Access Control Models and Technologies (SACMAT'06)*, pp. 139–149.

Schneider, F. B. (2000) „Enforceable Security Policies". *ACM Trans. Information and System Security*, 3(1):30–50.

Sekar, R., Venkatakrishnan, V. N., Basu, S., Bhatkar, S., and DuVarney, D. C. (2003) "Model-Carrying Code: A Practical Approach for Safe Execution of Untrusted Applications". In *Proc. 19th ACM Symposium on Operating Systems Principles (SOSP'03)*, pp. 15–28.

Shapiro, R. (2002) "A Comparison of XPDL, BPML, and BPEL4WS". http://xml.coverpages.org/ Shapiro-XPDL.pdf, last accessed 2012-01-20.

Sirer, E. G. and Wang, K. (2002) "An Access Control Language for Web Services". In *Proc. 7th Symposium on Access Control Models and Technologies (SACMAT'02)*, pp. 23–30.

Staab, S., Erdmann, M., and Maedche, A. (2000) "Semantic Patterns", Technical Report, AIFB, University of Karlsruhe, Germany.

Strembeck, M. and Mendling, J. (2011) "Modeling process-related RBAC models with extended UML activity models". *Inf. Softw. Technol.*, 53(5):456–483.

Swenson, K. (2008) "BPEL: Who needs it anyway?". bpm.com, http://bpm.com/bpel-who-needs-it.html, last accessed 2012-01-20.

Tai, S. (2011). "Cloud service engineering: a service-oriented perspective on cloud computing", In *Proc. 4th European conference on Towards a service-based internet (Service Wave'11)*. pp. 191–193.

Thatte, S. (2001) "XLANG Web Services for Business Process Design", Microsoft, 2001, http://xml.coverpages.org/XLANG-C-200106.html, last accessed: 2012-01-20.

Thompson, H. S., Beech, D., Maloney, M., and Mendelsohn, N., eds. (2004) "XML Schema Part 1: Structures Second Edition". World Wide Web Consortium, http://www.w3.org/TR/xmlschema-1/, last accessed: 2012-01-20.

Tuecke, S., Czajkowski, K., Foster, I., Frey, J., Graham, S., Kesselman, C., Maquire, T., Sandholm, T., Snelling, D., and Vanderbilt, P. (2003) "Open Grid Services Infrastructure (OGSI) Version 1.0". Global Grid Forum, GGF, http://www.ggf.org/documents/GWD-R/GFD-R.015.pdf, last accessed: 2012-01-20.

Vachharajani, N., Bridges, M. J., Chang, J., Rangan, R., Ottoni, G., Blome, J. A., Reis, G. A., Vachharajani, M., and August, D. I. (2004) "RIFLE: An Architectural Framework for User-Centric Information-Flow Security". In *Proc. the 37th International Symposium on Microarchitecture (MICRO-37'04)*, pp. 1–12.

Venkatakrishnan, V. N., Perit, R., and Sekar, R. (2002) "Empowering Mobile Code Using Expressive Security Policies". In *Proc. New Security Paradigms Workshop '02*, pp. 61–68.

Vigneras, P. (2008) "Why BPEL is not the holy grail for BPM". InfoQ, http://www.infoq.com/articels/bpelbpm, last accessed 2012-01-29.

Walker, D. (2000) "A type system for expressive security policies". In *Proc. 27th ACM SIGPLAN-SIGACT symposium on Principles of programming languages, POPL*, pp. 254–267.

Wang, H., Huang, J. Z., Qu, Y., Xie, J. (2004) "Web services: Problems and Future Directions". *Journal of Web Semantics*, 1(3):309–320.

Welch, V., Siebenlist, F., Foster, I., Bresnahan, J., Czajkowski, K., Gawor, J., Kesselman, C., Meder, S., Pearlman, L., and Tuecke, S., (2003) "Security for Grid Services", In *Proc. 12th IEEE International Symposium on High Performance Distributed Computing (HPDC'03)*, pp. 48–57.

Wijesekera, D. and Jajodia, S. (2003) "A Propositional Policy Algebra for Access Control". *ACM Trans. Information and System Security*, 6(2):286–325.

Wohed, P., van der Aalst, W. M, P., Dumas, M., and ter Hofstede, A. H. M. (2002) "Pattern-Based Analysis of BPEL4WS", Technical report, FIT-TR-2002-04, Queensland University of Technology, Brisbane, http://www.workflowpatterns.com/documentation/documents/qut_bpel_rep.pdf, last accessed 2012-01-20.

Workflow Management Coalition (2008) "Workflow Process Definition Interfaces XML Process Definition Language, Version 2.1a". http://www.wfmc.org/index.php?option=com_docman&task=doc_download&Itemid=72&gid=132, last accessed 2012-01-20.

Yoder, J. and Barcalow, J., (1997) "Architectural Patterns for Enabling Application Security", In *Proc. 4th Conference on Patterns Language of Programming (PLoP'97)*.

Index